ESSAYS OF U Ve Sa

TRANSLATION INITIATIVE OF THE TAMIL NADU TEXTBOOK AND EDUCATIONAL SERVICES CORPORATION

This is an initiative of the Tamil Nadu Textbook and Educational Services Corporation (TNTB & ESC) under the aegis of GO. Ms. No. 207, SE(TRB) Dept., Dated 22.09.2017, action plan 6, to identify and translate into English, Tamil literary works, that they might enhance the reach of Tamil antiquity, tradition and contemporaneity and enrich world literature to also translate significant literary voices for other languages into Tamil. Both ventures are to be undertaken as either an Independent or Joint publications with collaborating publishers.

ESSAYS OF
U Ve Sa

The man who revived Ancient Tamil Literature

Translated from Tamil by

Prabha Sridevan

Pradeep Chakravarthy

This book is being published under the Translation initiative of the Tamil Nadu Textbook and Educational Services Corporation

THORNBIRD

NIYOGI BOOKS

This book is being published under the Translation initiative of the Tamil Nadu Textbook and Educational Services Corporation

Published by
NIYOGI BOOKS
Block D, Building No. 77,
Okhla Industrial Area, Phase-I,
New Delhi-110 020, INDIA
Tel: 91-11-26816301, 26818960
Email: niyogibooks@gmail.com
Website: www.niyogibooksindia.com

Design: Shashi Bhushan Prasad

ISBN: 978-93-91125-54-7
Publication: 2022
Reprint: 2025

Printed at: Niyogi Offset Pvt. Ltd., New Delhi, India

Contents

Foreword
A world vision shaped by the love of language

U.Ve. Saminatha Iyer, more popularly known as U.Ve. Sa, lived for nearly a hundred years, spanning the latter part of the 19th century and the first part of the 20th (1855–1942). The world recognizes Tamil as a classical language today, mainly because he painstakingly collated, edited and published most of the Sangam literature that had been available only in palm-leaf manuscripts and lay scattered in different locations. He skilfully effected the technique of publishing and wrote detailed forewords and footnotes. In addition, he wrote his autobiography, biographies of others and his experiences as books and essays. His numerous writings have enriched the Tamil prose style, and he is therefore rightly acknowledged as Tamil Thatha.

Most of his writings are based on his own personal experience. He writes in a most entertaining style about what he has seen, heard and experienced. Every essay is about an incident. The structure is perfect, with a small introduction and a conclusion encapsulating his views. Many of his essays read like a story. Indeed, his essays have occasionally been included in collections of short fiction. This is because the incident described in them creates an illusion of fiction and draws the reader in.

Many scholars of ancient Tamil literature do not have a command over contemporary Tamil. And even if they did, their narrative style is not engrossing. But U.Ve. Sa had both command of language and style. He also understood perfectly what worked as an essay. The period during which he contributed articles to publication was about fifteen years at the most (1925–1942). Many magazines competed to publish his writings, because he had the ability to attract all types of readers. Moreover, he could recreate a fascinating picture of a past that everyone had thought was lost for ever.

U.Ve. Sa was not only an editor, but also a biographer and historian. He viewed everything as a source of history, and documented everything that came his way including oral records and traditions. He kept every letter he received, and used them as source material. Wherever he went, he noted down everything he saw, heard and learnt, and used them appropriately in his writings. He saw people as veritable treasure of information. He was not interested in those who had nothing to share or did not know how to share what they knew. It was his great disappointment that in Tamil, there was no reliable record of the lives of poets. He tried to make good that lapse, by collecting whatever data he could and documenting them. His writings never disappoint us; in each, there is at least one small detail that is new to the reader.

All his essays are based on records. In this translated collection, thirty essays have been selected from a wide spectrum of his writings. They include oral tales, autobiographical sketches, histories of places, life-stories and music-based essays. This collection contains a sample of all genres. He wrote many interesting essays on ancient Tamil literature. 'The Beggar's Song' relates how Chandrasekhara, a scholar, traced a stand-alone verse from a singing beggar. We are filled with amazement to read that even a beggar could sing ancient Tamil poetry, and also that a scholar followed that beggar to trace the poem for its merit. And we feel immensely proud to see how unparallelled riches of the Tamil language lay hidden in unexpected places and were handed down to posterity.

There is much to savour in every story in this collection. 'The Jasmine That Bloomed at Night' has a classic element; it not only relates how U.Ve. Sa searched for the manuscripts, but also other things, like how Tamil society protected the manuscripts, the traditions of the poet community and the culture of those times. 'The Legacy of Family Virtues' is also along the same lines. He has written many and diverse essays about his experiences as a lecturer in college. 'The Old Table' and 'My Experiences with Students' are two such, very interesting ones and useful in telling us how colleges functioned in those days.

'My Aim' is an essay which is vital to our understanding of him. He says his life's mission was to learn Tamil works in depth. He also gives us some guidelines to read old Tamil texts. It is the essence of what he learned by experience. He was a staunch Shaivite. But he understood that books based on Jainism and Buddhism, which were considered as alien religions during his time, were held in high esteem in ancient Tamil literature. He considered them as important sources of knowledge. So, he attempted to understand the basic tenets of those religions and made great efforts to publish the works. In 'My Aim', he says, 'It is wrong to condemn other religions and their gods. Understanding the basic principles of other religions and the uniqueness of other languages will widen our knowledge.' He also says that one must have a sense of affinity and solidarity with people belonging to other countries and other creeds, and be at peace with them. This is why he saw religion as a field of knowledge. U.Ve. Sa is an excellent example of how one's deep love for language and literature can expand their world vision.

It is a matter of joy that his writings are travelling across languages. He never projects himself, which is a remarkable trait. Even his autobiography mainly narrates the 19th-century tradition of scholars, the Tamil system of education and the publication of Tamil literature. The essays in this collection reflect the same trait. They reveal his mastery over language and also life in the Tamil region, and the fertility of ancient Tamil literature. I, therefore, consider it important that it is being retold in English. Judge Prabha Sridevan (retired) and Pradeep Chakravarthy have translated this collection. Mini Krishnan, who is responsible for the publication of this book, has worked hard to make Dravidian literature available in English. Tamil Nadu Textbook Education Services Corporation has led this project. My warm felicitations to all.

28 January 2021
பெருமாள் முருகன
நாமக்கல்

A Note from the Translators

It is our belief that U.Ve. Sa decided that this book should be written. It was sheer happenstance. We both met at Chitra Mahesh's place and somehow the conversation turned to how U.Ve. Sa's autobiography must be translated. We then realized that Sri K. Subramanian had already done an excellent job of that. U.Ve. Sa's many essays still remained unknown to many even if they have a connection to Tamil or Tamil Nadu.

The idea was not only to introduce U.Ve. Sa to a wider audience, but also to introduce the world U.Ve. Sa lived in. As the translation progressed, we saw more and more lucidly the world he had lived in, and the time spent in translation was almost equal to the time spent in talking to each other and sharing what we had read and how it had impacted us! Through his words, we glimpsed a bygone era so different from ours, but filled with people so familiar!

U.Ve. Sa's style is simple and almost conversational, and it was sheer pleasure transferring it into English. The world he writes of held some beautiful treasures that have been lost forever, and we do not mean tangible treasures, but intangible ones of human qualities that are in a way eternal. Or are they eternal? Some have vanished and some remain. In each of these stories, there are a few lessons for us to lead more fulfilling lives. We will let you draw your own conclusions!

We are happy that this volume will be a companion to Dr K. Subramanian's English translation of U.Ve. Sa's autobiography that reveals another side of U.Ve. Sa. Our choice of essays is purely personal. Perhaps, one day, all his essays (more than 400) and other writings will also be translated!

This has been a labour of love for both of us, punctuated by much laughter and introspection. We hope the essays leave you feeling just the same way! We are glad to have been able to execute this; it was the most useful way to spend the indefinite amount of time we had during the Covid 2020 lockdown.

Prabha had a personal angle to him as well. U.Ve. Sa held her great grandfather, V. Krishnaswami Iyer, in great regard. He even wrote an excellent tribute to him that has been adeptly translated by Dr Prema Nandakumar. In a way, she would like this collection to be a small but cherished "return gift" for that!

Many people helped us with this book. Sri. M.V. Pasupathy, a Tamil scholar, who worked for many years at the UV Swaminatha Library (USVL), introduced Pradeep to U.Ve. Sa, and loaned us his copies of the essay volumes. He is possibly the biggest expert on all things U.Ve. Sa today!

Dr V. Kadambari, Jayshree Kumar and Seetha Muthiah too gave us many useful suggestions. Thanks to Venkatesh Ramakrishnan and Karthik Bhatt for giving us many images connected to U.Ve. Sa.

We are very grateful to Perumal Murugan, himself an ardent admirer of U.Ve. Sa, for writing an excellent foreword for this volume. We are beholden to Mini Krishnan and the other members of the Tamil Nadu Text Book advisory committee for selecting this book for their project. In particular, we must mention Dr T.S. Saravanan, Deputy Director, Tamil Nadu Text Book and Educational Services Corporation.

Mini Krishnan's patient, sincere and tireless efforts to guide us through the translation process, her many pertinent suggestions to tighten the translation and honing to allow the words and the meaning to shine forth deserve a special appreciation with much gratitude.

We earnestly hope that anyone who has any connection with Tamil in any way will read this book, be grateful for what U.Ve. Sa has done for the language and use some nuggets of wisdom from these essays, for them to be as sincere, persistent and a timeless example of the way we should lead our lives. To quote from a verse he discovered—"it is because of such men, that this world still lives".

Justice Prabha Sridevan (Retired) and Pradeep Chakravarthy

Chennai

March 2021

U.Ve. Sa

Who was he?
Why should you know him?

Tamil is a classical language spoken by more than 80 million people across the world. It is one of India's Scheduled languages, and an official language in Sri Lanka and Singapore. In Malaysia, it is taught in schools. Tamil is also considered a classical language since it has literature dating back at least 2,000 years—much older than most other Indian languages and amongst the oldest languages in the world still actively in use.

Of the "classical" literature of Tamil Nadu, especially the Sangam poems, *Silappatikaram* and *Civaka Cintamani* (pronounced Seevaka Chintamani) are well known and have moved into English and other languages, the credit for rediscovering them, collating the multiple editions from palm leaf manuscripts, weeding out errors and publishing them as books in the late 19th and early 20th centuries goes entirely to U.Ve. Sa. If it were not for him, this corpus of literature that accords Tamil a classical status and has opened new doors to lovers of erudite literature would have rotted with the palm leaves they were written on, a century ago. It is in this context that he is affectionally and reverentially remembered as the "grandfather" of Tamil.

This book is a translation of a small selection of the 400-plus essays/speeches he has written. His autobiography *En Charitam* (My Story) began on 15 December 1939 as a column in the magazine, *Ananda Vikatan*, and continued till his demise on 28 April 1942.

He was born on 19 February 1855, in his mother Saraswathi's parental home in Sooryamoolai. His father Venkatasubbayyar hailed from Uthamadanapuram. His father had a small income from landholdings in his village and earned money by giving discourses. He was eternally paying off one debt of the loans taken by ancestors and worrying about meeting the expense of the next family function. Describing the village of more than hundred and seventy years ago, he says,

> There is a lot of difference in today's (1939) Uthamadanapuram and what I proudly refer to as 'Our Village'. It is the village of my early days that is enshrined in my mind. Many amenities of life today were absent then. No roads, no shops, no officials, no trundling sound of trains. However, there was beauty; there was peace; there was contentment among people; there was devotion. There was joy in their faces; and auspiciousness in their homes.[1]

1 English translation of *En Saritram*, K.S. Subramanian, p.11.

> There were traditional grants to the carpenters, blacksmiths, goldsmiths, fishermen, barbers and dhobis in Uthamadanapuram. They enjoyed these grants and performed their assigned roles efficiently. Some barbers were also knowledgeable in native medicine. They caringly treated the ailing persons by administering potions made out of herbs and other ingredients. For their treatment they charged a mere four annas (one anna was 1/16th of a Rupee) as their fee. One barber was also adept in surgical procedures. He had many ancient medical treatises. While these texts contained treatment regimens for different kinds of diseases, not all these diseases visited those patients.[2]

His autobiography gives us fascinating glimpses of the schooling system of those days and the popular games of the time. Much of his childhood was spent in Ariyaloor where his father was a musician in the Zamindar's court. He also began learning Tamil from Sadagopa Iyengar there. As the Zamindar's income dwindled and his father was worried about an ancestral debt of Rs 500, the family moved to a nearby place, Kunnam, where Chidambaram Pillai and other local Tamil lovers, funded the family. In addition to this, income came from gifts after discourses. They were, after harvest, also given *kambu* or pearl millet, *sorghum, samai* millet, ragi and *thinai* or Italian millet.

2 Ibid p.15.

He speaks about how while income was low, in villages in those days, those who were learned were always respected by everyone in the local community.

On 16 June 1868, he married Madurambikai from Malapuram. It is interesting to note that at this time, the groom's family bore the expenses for the wedding. His father gave the bride's father, Rs 200 for the wedding expenses, Rs 35 for the special wedding saree, Rs 150 for jewellery. The groom's family had to perform the *grihapravesam* ceremony and some other rituals for which an additional Rs 150 was needed and which was provided by a wealthy patron. The comments in the girl's family were, "The boy is good looking, has a luxurious tuft, sings well." The description of the wedding is fascinating: how they were unhurried affairs of bringing the family together over more than a month before the wedding itself which was spread over four days. We also learn that the concept of a morning coffee was unknown in those days.

It was about this time that he came to know of Thyagaraja Chettiar who was teaching Tamil in the Government Arts College, Kumbakonam, and his teacher, the great scholar, Sri Meenakshi Sundaram Pillai. U.Ve. Sa's love for Tamil was so great that when a friend of his father, Venkat Rao, a lawyer in Kumbakonam said, "What is the use of learning Tamil in this day and time? Why take all this trouble? Ask him to leave it all aside and make him learn English. I'll help him; I'll also request my friends to contribute. He will truly progress in life in a few years." U.Ve. Sa was only angry that he was being dissuaded when the request was to get an introduction to Thyagaraja Chettiar.

To enable his education in Tamil, the family moved to Chenganam for him to study under the scholar Vridachala Reddiar. After some time, at his suggestion, they journeyed to Mayuram to meet the great Pillai himself. Describing his first meeting with his teacher in 1871, U.Ve. Sa wrote:

> I was struck by the savant's appearance. He came majestically like a sauntering elephant. A sumptuous presence, an emerging paunch, long arms reaching up to the knees, broad forehead, a small tuft, a pure white dhoti—all these pointed to traditional wealth. Even so, his face lacked the bloom of a rich person; had the tranquil poise of a deep and expansive ocean sans waves. His eyes were not marked by penetrating severity; nor studied disdain; they gently caressed whatever they touched.

After a meeting of much anxiety for U.Ve. Sa, he was taken in as a student and began classes with Pillai. Several pages of his autobiography are dedicated to the love and affection that the student and teacher developed for each other. Their trips to many parts of Tamil Nadu are glimpses of an era we can only imagine. It was Pillai who gave him the name Saminatha. In 1874, he began writing his first book and till 31 January, when his teacher passed away, they were inseparable. U.Ve. Sa continued to serve the Tiruvavaduthurai Adheenam as a Tamil scholar and in 1880, with the efforts of Thyagaraja Chettiar, became a Tamil teacher in the Kumbakonam College as a replacement for Chettiar. Very soon, he was blessed with a son. It was during this stay that there occurred a fateful meeting that was to alter U.Ve. Sa's life forever.

He had settled into his job in the college and was also taking extra classes. Salem Ramaswami Mudaliar had recently been transferred as Munsif of Kumbakonam. U.Ve. Sa was asked by the Tiruvavaduthurai Adheenam to meet him since it was said that Mudaliar was a keen Tamil scholar. On a Thursday, 21 October 1880, U.Ve. Sa met him and informed him that both his previous position in the Adheenam and his current position in the college were that of a Tamil teacher. U.Ve. Sa was mildly puzzled about his indifference. Then even when U.Ve. Sa mentioned his illustrious teacher, Mudaliar was not impressed. "Even after speaking about Pillai, this person shows no enthusiasm. Is he really keen on Tamil?" thought U.Ve. Sa to himself with a touch of irritation. In response to Mudaliar's question—"What books have you read?"—U.Ve. Sa rattled off more than a hundred works from different genres in the hope that he would overwhelm him.

"What is the use of studying all this?" Mudaliar sharply interjected. U.Ve. Sa was disappointed and wondered whether he was expecting English texts.

U.Ve. Sa continued with a much longer list and ended with the Kamba Ramayana, but Mudaliar still asked, "Is that all?" U.Ve. Sa was perplexed.

"What about the ancient texts?"

U.Ve. Sa writes that he was surprised that in all his deep study and teaching, he had not even heard of the texts that he mentioned—*Silappatikaram, Civaka Cintamani* and *Manimekalai.* U.Ve. Sa promised to read them if he could see a copy. The next Sunday, Mudaliar gave him a copy of a part of the *Civaka Cintamani* and narrated the curious way in which he stumbled upon it and how no Tamil scholar had ever gone beyond the puranic texts.

Starting with the first verse, U.Ve. Sa tells us the fascinating story of how he rediscovered this great Tamil Jain epic, and encountered the problems of missing verses, conflicting commentaries and above all, his own understanding of an entirely different faith. U.Ve. Sa was entranced by the love Mudaliar had for the epic and as more and more unfamiliar words popped up, U.Ve. Sa's persistence overtook him. Starting with visiting Jains in Kumbakonam, his thirst to read and thoroughly understand this Jain epic soon became an all-consuming passion. A Jain woman, Tharani Chettiar, calls him a *bhavya jeevan* or a person ready for benediction and this seems to be an apt first step for U.Ve. Sa to have started his life-long journey to publish ancient Tamil works which made him immortal for lovers of Tamil today. As a Shaivite who had learnt of the Chola king being "in love with this heretical text", U.Ve.

Sa now, as he became more and more engrossed in the text, began to savour the beauty and depth of meaning of this ancient Tamil composition.

At that time, Mudaliar resigned and moved to Chennai. When they parted, U.Ve. Sa promised Mudaliar that he would not let this epic die in oblivion, but would get other versions, edit them and publish the complete edition.

The remaining 272 pages of his autobiography detail the enormous pains he took to source the manuscripts, the occasions when he was too late to save the manuscripts from being disposed as garbage and how, in this search, he found greater riches like the other epics—*Silappatikaram*, *Manimekalai*, almost found *Valayapathi* but was disappointed, and the great treasure of Sangam poems—the *Agananuru* and the *Purananuru*. While talking about *Valayapathi*, U.Ve. Sa says, he had himself seen it in the Adheenam library, but when he went again to search for it, it had gone missing. Speaking of his feelings, he says, borrowing from Kamban's lines, it was like a visually challenged person who regained his sight only to lose it again.

He went from village to village, spending his resources and time, and persuaded people to introduce him to local Tamil scholars or their descendants. Sifting through the palm leaves, often in vain, and when he got the texts, comparing them, deleting extraneous text, finding wealthy sponsors to publish them as books became his life's passion and mission. We hear nothing much of his family life, but his movement from Kumbakonam to Chennai and naming his house, purchased in 1909, in gratitude, after his teacher Thyagaraja Chettiar. This has been razed to the ground and does not exist now.

Civaka Cintamani was published in 1887 and he kept his promise to Mudaliar, who passed away in 1892. About the challenges he faced, he wrote:

> I also referred to the difficulties I encountered while examining and comparing different textual versions. Many were the difficulties I had to face during the long journey of determining the correct final text and the related clear meanings of the commentaries. Untiring study and frequent textual comparisons of many ancient and damaged palm (leaf) script copies had to be undertaken. Letter and word were often wrongly spelt, repeated, omitted or reversed; the commentary itself had to be carefully analysed to distinguish what was the detailed gloss and what a mere paraphrase. To determine where a quotation commenced and when it ended; to recognise how the paraphrase had to be linked to the related text; to identify an error as an error and to decide to discard it; the daunting effort of correctly interpreting the meaning in the middle of a maze of confusion. I had to put the supreme effort to evolve order out of chaos. Even with all these efforts a few portions

> defied clarity. This was mainly caused by the absence today of the ancient Tamil texts related to Music and Drama referred to in the text.[3]

The full complexity and arduousness of this will dawn on us only when we learn that, in addition to this, he had to—with primitive travel facilities—search for these in every village, often times spending a few days in a home sifting through manuscripts and finding nothing or just a few leaves, a part of a text and seldom a full manuscript. All his work was done completely manually, mostly by him, with the assistance of a few students. The content was also new to him. For the Jain epics, he could reach out to a few Tamil Jains, but for *Manimekalai*, the Buddhist work, there was no Tamil Buddhist to help him since the practice of Buddhism had gone extinct in Tamil Nadu for several centuries. After publication, there were his critiques and the small extract below of how he handled them is a lesson in our age of fragile egos:

> When Chintamani was published, there was very little exposure of such works in Tamil Nadu. When a work is published in the face of considerable difficulties, in such an atmosphere, it is natural for a few errors to creep in. In the matter of publication of ancient texts, it is not uncommon for each succeeding edition to incorporating corrections to faulty readings,

3 Ibid p.710.

> incorporating fresh insights, into the true meaning and also to providing additional new information. It is simply not possible to produce a perfect edition straightaway. I have myself corrected many errors in the first edition of my book, in subsequent editions. Based on the knowledge gained from new research, persisting wrong understanding also gets corrected. For has not Tiruvalluvar said, "*aridho rariyamai kandatral* (One's ignorance is discovered the more one learns)?
>
> There were errors in my Chintamani edition because of my ignorance. ... Likewise, many mistakes in respect of names of books and the names of poets appear in the first edition of Chintamani, I gradually corrected these errors. The reading we adopt as correct today may subsequently be found faulty and we adopt a new reading. How can we at all declare as full and final any work of research based on man's limited knowledge?[4]

In 1898, the Tamil Buddhist epic *Manimekalai* was published. Because he had to find sponsors to publish the books, these publications were usually delayed. While he never responded to critics, he would accommodate their views (when accurate) into the future editions.

In 1903, he moved to Chennai to teach in the Presidency College and on 1 January 1906, he received the title of

4 Ibid p.766.

Mahamahopadhyaya, had a conversation with the then Governor and received an award of a thousand rupees. In 1911, he received a coronation pension of Rs 100 (annual) and in 1912, the Governor attended his Tamil class for about 1 ½ hours. On 8 May 1917, he lost his wife. In 1919, he met Rabindranath Tagore who composed a poem on him[5]. Publications of other works followed, the *Kurunthokai*, the *Perun Kathai*, the *Puraporul Venba Malai* and many others. From 15 December 1939, he began writing his autobiography for Ananda Vikatan magazine. On 13 January 1942, he stumbled and fell in his home. He seems to have recovered somewhat and fearing the bombing of Chennai in the World War, moved to Tirukazhukundram. On 27 April 1942, he was afflicted by high fever, and at about 3:35 pm the next day, he passed away. Even though it was war time, tributes poured in. On 5 July 1947, his entire book collection was opened up as the UVSL, under the patronage of Rukmini Devi's Kalakshetra, where it continues to exist. In 1948, a statue of him was installed in Presidency College, Chennai (then Madras).

Unfortunately, not a single university in Tami Nadu bears his name, and one wonders if those who still study the great epics or the ancient Tamil verses spare a moment to think of the stupendous struggle he went through to save, retrieve and revive them, making them known to the world.

---

5 Retrieved on 19 April 2020 from https://timesofindia.indiatimes.com/blogs/tracking-indian-communities/tagores-ode-hailed-tamil-savant/

Translators like A.K. Ramanujan gave him credit, but the thousands of children who study Tamil or study in Tamil—it is unlikely that they will know who "Tamil Thatha" was, let alone why he came to be called so. However, it is very likely that U.Ve. Sa would only tell us, "What did I do? I only did my duty to my elders and Tamil by collecting, editing and publishing these ancient works for future generations. There is no need to praise me or remember me for just doing my duty!"

References

Iyer, U.Ve. Saminatha. 2019. *The Story of My Life*. Trans. K.S. Subramanian. New Delhi: Sahitya Akademi.

My Aim[1]

It is easy to ask someone, "What is your aim?" But it is a very difficult question to answer. The editor of *Kalaimagal* requested me to write a few lines about my aim in life. I thought to myself, "What is the point of writing about my aim? If we understand the thoughts of great people and follow them, that will benefit us." However, I could not refuse a request made by someone who holds me in high regard, so I have attempted to answer his question.

All my aims in life are somehow connected to Tamil: to read Tamil texts deeply and several times, so that they reveal their many layers of meanings. It will be difficult in the beginning, but if we persist, gradually we will be able to understand them. As we read a text, we must enjoy the writing style *and* the meaning. We must also talk and write about them, sharing in a way that others enjoy them as much as we did.

Old texts must be read thoroughly and understood. We must not pretend we know what we have not understood.

1 Originally published in Tamil journal, *Kalaimagal*, March 1935.

We must take good care of the texts. We must not extrapolate new meanings into them. It is unnecessary to add to the meaning or commentary in order to extract appreciation. Should we find errors of words or meaning in old texts, we must first do a thorough research on why they may have crept in. Merely because we have not understood something should not cause us to decide that it is an error. There is no use in hastily concluding that we are correct and deriding others. We must focus only on the good part that is useful for us and take that up and not criticize it.

We must learn from well-qualified scholars, listen and learn carefully and teach others accurately and thoughtfully. Nothing can be better than this. We must constantly update our knowledge by reading.

Following what our ancients did is the best way for mental peace. We must research and fully understand new ideas, new faiths and new gods, before we choose to follow them; this is the best way to be at peace and harmony with ourselves. If we ignore this, it will disturb the unity of people. We must not insult other religions and gods. Learning more about the beliefs of other religions and rare insights found in other languages will help broaden our minds.

We must live in fraternity and harmony with people from other countries or faiths.

All the above suggestions must be carefully analyzed and incorporated bit by bit, slowly and perfectly. If people discourage us, we must not relent, but continue. There is no doubt that if we do our duty and persist with what we consciously and sincerely believe is right, Divinity will help us to succeed. Rather than singing our own praises, we should allow our results to speak for us.

It is best to forget the insults we endure from others and advisable not to share them. Never forget to express gratitude even for the smallest act of kindness. It is gratitude that makes us human.

Older people may not have read like us, but their habits will hold us in good stead. Sri Subramania Desikar of Tiruvavaduthurai Adheenam, who hailed from Melagaram, would often say this when he headed the monastery.

Our destiny is predetermined by our actions and the divine. It is unwise to stoke the fire of anger in our heart against those who have acted against us. That God will do only good for us must be a firm belief. This belief will be a bulwark against the many difficulties life will present us with.

These are but a few precepts from my experience with elders and in life. I earnestly attempt to live by them.

The *Kural* (or the *Tirukural*) says, "He who desires not pleasure but labour, will be a pillar to sustain his relatives and wipe away their sorrows."

The Field that Fed[1]

When I lived in Kumbakonam, I once wanted to attend the Sapthasthana festival in Tiruvaiyaru. The festival occurs on a full moon day, in the month of Chithirai (April 15–May 15). This incident happened more than fory-five years ago.

I left the previous day and got off at Ayyanpettai railway station, and proceeded along the banks of the Kaveri river. On my way, there were many temple towns. I stopped at each of them and found out all the stories and legends connected with them. Whichever town I visited, I would learn about the stories of the poets, patrons, the hagiology, the stories that had been preserved orally, and carefully note them down. Because of these notes, I was able to understand many rare facts unknown to me for long years.

On my path was a temple town called Tiru Chotruthurai. It is now called Tiru Chaththurai. It finds a place in the Tevaram hymns. In Sanskrit, it is called *odhanavanam*. The name of Lord Shiva in the temple is Odhanavaneswarar and

1 Originally published in the Tamil journal, *Kalaimagal*, in December 1937.

his consort is called Annapoorni. It is one of the Saptasthana[2] temples connected with Tiruvaiyaru. I had heard other legends about it. Since Gautama Rishi had performed penance there, it was also called Gautamashrama.

It is said that during a prolonged drought, the Goddess herself had distributed food to the poor people. In fact, it seems that cooked rice had appeared instead of paddy in some fields. I had heard that even today there is evidence of this and I was keen to learn more.

I stopped many passers-by and asked them questions about the history and stories of the place. Some did not answer, and others asked me to direct these questions to the temple priest. It looked as if they thought, that barring the temple priest no one knew details about the temple.

I went to the Agraharam[3] area of the village. There was a house with a tiled roof. I stood outside and looked at the people inside who were busy. They were serving food to several pilgrims, who were on the way to attend the Sapthasthana festival in Tiruvaiyaru.

"Is anyone home?" I asked from the street.

"Who is outside? Do you need water?" asked a man as he came out of the house with a pot of water. He must have assumed I would want water!

I accepted the water gratefully, and said, "I want other things too."

---

2 Seven Shiva temples in and around Tiruvaiyaru on the banks of the Kaveri that are connected to each other through rituals.

3 The area where Brahmins used to reside.

"What else?" he said, looking a little puzzled.

I replied, "Not much; I want to know more about the temple. I believe the Goddess fed everyone in the village. Can you tell me more?"

"What else is there to say? You have said everything yourself!"

"Can you point me to some evidence of this? I will be grateful."

"I don't know about all that," he said, and went inside to attend to his work.

"Who is that, *ayya*?"—I heard a voice. Since I was standing in the sun and was tired, I could not see clearly and thus hesitated.

"What do you want to know, *ayya*?" The question was repeated. I turned around, and close to me, on the *thinnai* of the house was a very old woman, sitting with her legs stretched out.

"Were you talking to me?" I asked as I approached her.

"Yes," she said.

She appeared to be more than eighty years old, and was sightless. Around her were a stout walking stick and a few torn rags; in a coconut husk were a few pebbles to help her do her *japa*, a discoloured metal *chombu* and a small tin vessel with a lid that held some eatables. There was what looked like a screen on which was hung a shabby white saree, washed and left to dry. She was chewing something and moving her pebbles as she was mentally doing her *japa*.

"You asked something to the people inside. What was it?" she asked me, on hearing the sound of my footsteps.

"I asked about this town and its temple."

"Oh, come, sit beside me. They won't know anything about such things. The women there only know how to braid and adorn their hair with flowers. What temple? What temple tank? Only I know such things. Did they respond to your questions?"

I confessed they hadn't.

"See, I told you they would not know. Why did you go and ask them in the first place? Who takes notice of me these days? All that they do is give me food at mealtimes. Who asks my advice for anything? Were the old days like this?"

The old lady took a pause for a while. Clearly, she had transported herself to the old days. She came back to the present.

"Let the child get fever, then this *paati* will be needed. For advice on medicines, tablets and the herbs, she will be needed. Anyway, let that pass, now tell me, which town are you from?"

"Uthamadanapuram."

"Oh, of course, we have relatives there too. What jati are you?"

"Ashtasahasram."

"*Adey*! We are the same! Who is your father?"

I told her. I wanted to reach Tiruvaiyaru quickly, after collecting the information about the temple and the legends, but I could not escape her questions and was forced to oblige her. What to do?

"My father's grandmother's mother-in-law is from this village," I told the old lady.

"Very good. You and I may even be related; I am sure, if we dig a bit deeper, we will find a connection. But in today's world, where is there a need for relatives, kin and people? Is it like the old days? The white man has given us the railways. We make alliances in Bombay and Calcutta, but we don't know or even care about our own close family who live next to us."

The old lady was enthused. Obviously, no one chatted with her. One by one, she took out long buried thoughts and opinions. I was her captive and patient listener.

I could have quietly slipped away, but my heart did not permit that. I was reminded of a proverb on being persistent, if we chew one measure of husk, we may get at least one flattened rice. My interactions with old people have always been profitable in learning many new facts and anecdotes, so I gave her a patient hearing and responded to her politely and respectfully.

In a short while, I had to tell her about my village, caste, clan, *gotra*, occupation, salary, marriage, children, family details and many other things. I eventually realized that if this continued, her interrogation would be endless and gently reminded her, "Now please tell me about this village."

"Yes, yes. I haven't forgotten, let me tell you. Once during a great drought, our Goddess fed the village in a large field that still stands," she said. "It is called the Annam Padaitha Vayal (the field that fed)."

When the conversation had gone the way I wanted and I had got the information I needed, I forgot about having spent so much time with her.

"Where is it?" I asked eagerly.

"If I could see, I could have told you," she said and gave me the directions and features of the location instead.

"To the south of this village is a canal called Sorudaiyan. Sorudaiyan is also the name of our deity." This was a new piece of information. As the sightless old lady continued sharing such nuggets one by one, I kept listening intently and storing them safely in my memory. In between, she gave me a lot of irrelevant information, which I instantly forgot.

"In these days, who listens to such ancient information? Even if people wanted to know, who is there to tell them? Only some old piece of wood (implying herself) will keep chattering about this." She sighed sadly. I could sense her self-pity. I listened to the chatter of this "old piece of wood" and noted it down later. It would have been impossible to get it from another source.

"Do you want to know anything else?" she asked.

She was not tired at all and was willing to say more. I, however, had to reach Tiruvaiyaru before dusk and respectfully, took leave.

Involuntarily, I developed a sense of affection and respect for her. I felt an inexplicable sadness too. There are many "old pieces of wood" like her who had much to share, but had no listeners, and died with their knowledge and memories deeply buried in their hearts.

Note: After I shared this with the Raja's college Tamil professor Sriman T.G. Somasundara Desikar, he added the following information.

This village is mentioned in the Tiruvaiyaru Puranam. The village in that text is called Annavadhara Sthalam. Gautama Rishi had performed penance there. There was a drought for 12 years. Hearing his prayers, Shiva caused the fields to grow rice that Gautama distributed to the starving residents. To the southwest of the temple's lily pond are some fields that are the ones mentioned in the story. Sorudaiyan Canal is now called Sodaran Canal.

The Legacy of Family Virtues

I can never forget Mithilaipatti. I wrote this in my foreword to *Manimekalai*:

> It is the Mithilaipatti manuscript alone which was the oldest copy (of this epic), indispensable to my research, and which helped in organising incomplete, faulty and error-laden parts in the other copies, so that the ornament (*manimekalai*-waistlet) that had lost its beauty, and was dust-laden and misaligned was made worthy of being worn by the Goddess of Tamil herself.

There are many sacred places in Tamil Nadu: Shiva, Vishnu and Subramania shrines. According to me, Mithilaipatti is one of the important shrines where the Tamil Goddess resides. It belongs to the Shivagangai principality. It is a few miles from Tirumeyyam in Pudukkottai. I collected some manuscripts from there, and the person who helped, Azhagiya Sitrambala Kavirayar, is dear to me. He came from a family of Tamil scholars who had, for generations, guarded several rare Tamil manuscripts in their home. His ancestors had received many royal gifts like elephants and other endowments. In this house, I have seen the stone which elephants used to be tied to in the olden days, and the howdah. It appeared as if the place was filled with the blessings of both the goddesses of wealth and learning. Azhagiya Sitrambala Kavirayar, a wealthy man, shared many anecdotes about his ancestors when I spent time with him and also recounted some of his own experiences. Here's an account of one such incident:

Once he had to go to distant Oroor, to attend a wedding. He fixed a bullock-cart for the all-night return trip. The cart-man asked for three rupees; in addition, since it would be morning when they reached their destination, he bargained for a meal on arrival. Kavirayar agreed.

When they set off at night, Kavirayar lay down to sleep. The moonlight was bright and the cart-man drove on happily singing Themmangu[1] and other songs. The bullocks sped along. Kavirayar appreciated his songs. Then the cart man gently asked him about his family. Kavirayar began his story.

"I live in Mithilaipatti. My ancestors were highly educated and wrote books and received many awards. At first, they resided in Oroor, in Salem district. They were patronized by one Kattiyappa Mudaliar who sponsored religious services at the Taramangalam temple. This Mithilaipatti village was given as a gift to one of my ancestors (Azhagia Sitrambala Kavirayar) by Vengalappa Naicker, who was a zamindar of that region. The document recording this gift is in our house.

1 Songs usually sung during a journey.

My ancestors received many gifts from the Ramanathapuram Sethupathi, the zamindars of Marungapuri and the Shivagangai rulers. In those days, kings and zamindars understood the greatness of Tamil and nurtured Tamil pundits. So, these scholars also enjoyed a good life like the nobility. At present, our sustenance is this Mithilaipatti, gifted to us by that Vengalappa Naicker, on whose magnanimity we live, and that is what keeps our families in comfort. Are you listening?"

"Yes, please continue."

"Vengalappa Naicker's charity and his fame are undiminished. The descendants of those patronized by him like us and others are well off today. They gave boundless wealth to others like they gave to my forefathers. Their family earned eternal fame by their unstinted munificence. Later, however, that family split up, and their wealth dwindled. Today, I do not even know, where and in what condition his descendants are. The wheel of time keeps turning." Azhagiya Sitrambala Kavirayar was tired after narrating this and went to sleep. The cart reached Mithilaipatti early next morning. Kavirayar reached home. He bade his servant to give the cart-man some food, but the cart man did not want any and said he would like to leave right away.

"But it will be a long while before you reach your place. Eat something." Kavirayar insisted.

"I am not hungry now. On the way, I will eat at some acquaintance's house."

"Fine, please take your fare for the trip."

"No, please keep the money. I'm leaving." The cart man said respectfully.

Kavirayar was startled, he thought that the cart-man expected more money.

"But you agreed to three rupees, is it not?"

"Please, *ayya*? I will go, do not misunderstand me," he said with an air of noble dignity.

"Why, *appa*, I cannot understand you." Kavirayar said kindly.

"*Ayya,* last night you spoke of your forefathers, I am a descendant of that Vengalappa Naicker who was your family's patron. It is my sad lot that I am now a driver of carts. My elders have taught me never to take back what was gifted by us. My conscience doesn't permit me to take even a small bit from you which was given by my forefathers. Excuse me please. It is my good fortune that by God's grace I was of some use to you." Before Kavirayar could say a word, he drove off.

Kavirayar kept thinking of his noble demeanour, the greatness of Vengalappa Naicker's family and felt sorry for the cartman's present state. His eyes filled with tears.

Even when he told me this story many years later, as he came to this last scene, his voice choked and his eyes were wet.

The greatness and magnanimity of the people who are born in good families will never diminish. *Kettalum men makkal men makkaley*—noble people remain noble even in adversity. Can there be a better example to explain this wise adage?

The Night Jasmine

In 1887, I was working hard on researching and publishing the *Civaka Cintamani* for the first time. I noticed the mention of several other books and of the existence of several ancient Tamil books. The anthology of ten texts, was called *Pathu Paattu,*[1] which included a work called the *Tiru Murugattruppadai.* I grew keen to acquire these ten songs and read and research them thoroughly. With the help of several friends, I was able to acquire some copies of this text. However, they did not contain all the ten songs. Even among those that were available, some were on highly damaged palm leaves; some had the song, but no commentary. Others had the commentary, but not the song. The text of some had many mistakes. I continued my search for the ten songs.

When I was working in the Kumbakonam College I used to spend my vacation searching for these songs. There

1 The ten texts in the anthology were: *Tiru Muragattrupadai, Porunarattrupadai, Cirrupanaatrupadai, Perumbanaatrupadai, Mullai Paatu, Madurai Kanchi, Nedunalvaadai, Kurinchipaattu, Pattinapalai and Malaipadukadam.*

was a week's holiday for Aavani Avittam[2] and I thought this was a good opportunity to travel to Tirunelveli and search in the homes of hereditary scholars for good copies of this text. That vacation, I decided to visit Tirunelveli and the Azhwar Tirunagari area and contacted a few friends there.

My father said, "In this auspicious time, why do you want to travel? Stay here and go there on your next vacation."

I gave him many reasons, but he did not relent. However, since the anthology was more important than the auspicious week, I was, with great difficulty, able to convince him and leave. At 8 in the evening, I got into a single bullock cart to go to the railway station. My father bid me a half-hearted goodbye. I had a tin trunk with me. When we were going south of the Vaanathurai, the cart hit something and toppled. I fell down and my trunk fell over me. I did not give up even then. My mind was already in Tirunelveli. If a saint had given me a teleporting pill, saying that I could have used it in an emergency, I would have used it right then! My mind was fast, but my cart was slow and this accident made it worse.

I considered returning and restarting the next day. If I did so, my father would use this ill omen to stall the trip and, therefore, I decided to continue. So, after paying the full fare to the cart-man, I picked up my trunk and rushed to the station, and was lucky to catch my train. After crossing Thanjavur, the train stopped near a forest. Several officials came and inspected the train for a long time. I was groggy

2 Ritual practiced by Brahmins when they change their sacred thread.

with sleep as they ordered us to change compartments since the one in front of mine had caught fire. They had decided to detach both the compartments. I prayed and got into another compartment. I was disturbed that there were so many hurdles. However, my good cheer soon returned and I was excited about the trip.

I reached Tirunelveli the next day. At that time, a Kanakasabhai Mudaliar was the Sub-Judge there. He was my friend from his days in Thanjavur and was transferred to Tirunelveli later. He was aware of my interest in old Tamil manuscripts, and through K. Sundaram Iyer, had promised to help me source such manuscripts in that region. Since I remembered that offer, and I had written to him before the trip, I went to his house.

Without even asking about my travel, he said, "I had just written a letter to you and was about to post it. Here, please read it," and thrust a letter into my hands. It had even been addressed to me and stamped. I opened it and read the contents.

I am unable to help you in your search for old texts as I had promised. Another childhood friend of mine, Sri C.V. Damodaran Pillai, had made a similar request and I had promised to assist him. He has asked for the same texts as you. Therefore I cannot help you. Don't trouble yourself to come here.

"That is fine. I came only because you promised to help me. If you will not, there are many patrons and scholars who will willingly do it. Thank you."

Mudaliar must have thought I would be crestfallen; my response astonished him.

"Really? You know people and places here? Who are they? Where do you intend to go?" He asked me.

"In this region, I will get the support of many wealthy persons. Several zamindars are known to me. Azhwar Tirunagari, Sri Vaikuntam and Thenthiruperai are places I intend to visit."

I also gave him the names of several people in high office, who were outside his control and circle of influence. Mudaliar requested me to share what I had got, so that he could share them with Damodaran Pillai.

"I myself am running hither and thither and you want me to share what I get? You are a man in high office; with your influence, you can get many more texts." I laughed and took leave of him.

I then went to the house of the well-known lawyer and philanthropist A. Krishnaswami Iyer in Kailasapuram. He welcomed me.

He asked, "When did you arrive here? Couldn't you have informed me earlier?"

I told him of my desire to go to Azhwar Tirunagari to visit the homes of some Tamil poets and scholars for their old palm leaf manuscripts.

"Don't worry! My friend Subbaraya Mudaliar is a well-known lawyer in Sri Vaikuntam. I will write a letter of introduction for you; he will do the needful." He also arranged a cart to take me there.

In Sri Vaikuntam, I was received with affection by Subbaraya Mudaliar. He promised to help me. I went with him to nearby Azhwar Tirunagari. When I went there, my friends to whom I had written awaited my arrival. I had a letter from Sri Ambalavana Desikar, the head of the Tiruvavaduthurai *matha*, to the head of a *matha* in Azhwar Tirunagari to help me. They had already collected all the old manuscripts from the local poets and kept them ready for me.

I first went to Lakshmana Kavirayar's house. He was from the lineage of the great Teeratha Vinai Theertha Tirumeni Kavirayar. His library had several thousand manuscripts. There were works of grammar, religious poems, puranas and other old books. I checked them thoroughly, but the ten songs I wanted were not there. One manuscript had a list of more than 30,000 texts. From that list, was one book, which contained the first seven songs in the anthology. I had had nothing but ill omens on this trip till now, but with this good omen, my confidence returned! My hope was that I would now find the ten songs in this library.

I was in Azhwar Tirunagari for three days. The first day was Aavani Avittam. My host was the local school examiner and friend Sivarama Iyer in nearby Sri Vaikuntam. My day would be spent in the library of Lakshmana Kavirayar. During a break, I would be at the libraries of other local poets—Thai Avalam Theertha Kavirayar, Amrutha Kavirayar, and others. I searched in the homes of thirty poets; I searched all the manuscripts in Lakshmana Kavirayar's house; but I could not find what I had come for. The ill omens had not been wrong, I told myself with a heavy heart.

Lakshmana Kavirayar told me, “In my house, there were countless manuscripts. Among my ancestors, were three brothers, and when one of them died, his wife decided to return to her home in Thatchanallur. At that time, she took her husband’s share of manuscripts.”

I said, “The ten anthologies may have been in that set. All our efforts have been in vain.”

Suddenly, a thought occurred to him and he told me, “Something has slipped my mind. My father-in-law, Devapiran Pillai, lives here. I am not on good terms with him. One of my servants had given him some of my manuscripts. You may check those, but I am not in touch with him.”

I supplicated and said, “For my sake and for the sake of Tamil, can you please set aside your differences and arrange to have those texts brought here, I am also willing to come with you.” Others around him also requested him and Lakshmana Kavirayar agreed.

My hands and my heart were sore with sifting through so many manuscripts, and that too in vain. I visited the residence of the Sub Registrar of the village—Ramasami Iyer. At night, after dinner at his place, I sat on the *thinnai* of his home. Some of the Sri Vaishnava scholars acceded to my request and narrated some old commentaries of some of the *Divya Prabandham* verses. I listened to them with great interest and joy, but I did not get the full satisfaction I would have normally got. It was not their fault; it was because of my trepidation for I had not found the ten anthologies.

That evening, there was a temple procession. The deity, and the Azhwar who was born in that town, were being taken in procession. Respectfully, we rose and offered our prayers. Due to the love and affection of all those around me, the priests honoured me with flowers, a garland and the sandal paste of the deities.

I looked at the image of Nammazhwar and said from my heart, "Swami, you are known as the person who created the Tamil Veda. I have come to your town in search of a Tamil book. You, who have given such glory to Tamil, don't you know my difficulties? It is unfair, that you don't have the mercy to endow me with success in this endeavor." This plea flowed from my dejection. I had reconciled myself to my fate and decided there was nothing more I could do.

The deities and the procession passed us and we sat down again. In the bright moonlight I saw Lakshmana Kavirayar hurrying towards us with something covered in his upper cloth. I thought it was some food offering from the temple.

He gave me some manuscripts wrapped in the cloth, saying, "Please look! I told him I would return it after checking." In my eagerness, I snatched the bunch from him before he could hand it over.

I untied the rope and opened the palm leaf manuscript. In the moonlight, I saw the words "Mullai Pattu" or Jasmine Songs, right on top.

Truly, this was a jasmine that had bloomed in the moonlight. Seeing this, my heart bloomed (this was one of the ten anthologies). I was overjoyed; swiftly, I went through it again and again. The first was *Tirumurugatrupadai*, then *Porunaratrupadai, Sirupanatrupadai*, and so on until *Nedunelvadai*. The manuscript had seven of the songs. I lost myself in joy as I studied the manuscript many times over. My ecstasy knew no bounds! If someone had seen me that day for the first time, they would have thought I was a mad man! My mind was so feverish!

My prayers to Azhwar had not been in vain. He is a god indeed, I told those around me. I could not sleep that night. Next morning, I performed a small puja in the temple for the Vishnu deity and Azhwar, and sought their continued blessings in my work.

I gave to Lakshmana Kavirayar *Civaka Cintamani* and other books that I had taken with me, and requested him to give it to the zamindar of Uthumalai, Hridayalaya Marudappa Thevar. Along with the *Pathu Pattu*, in his library, I got a few pages of the *Ainkurunuru* with an old but incomplete commentary, *Pathirrupathu* and the manuscripts of *Puraporul Venba Malai*. I took leave of my friends and visited a few other poets and their libraries, and returned to Tirunelveli.

There, I met Kanakasabhai Mudaliar again. He asked me where I had been, whom I had met and what I had found. I responded to these questions. He asked whether I could give some of them to him to give to his friend Damodaran Pillai.

I asked him, "How will I give you what I found with so much physical, mental and emotional effort? Is it fair of you to profit from the effort of others, without lifting a little finger?" He made no reply.

I then visited Krishnaswami Iyer in Kailasapuram, thanked him and returned to Kumbakonam. The manuscript I had received in the moonlight had the commentaries for only seven songs, but they were accurate.

I have had many arduous experiences in locating old manuscripts. This is one of them.

A Poor Person's Love for Tamil

Once, a wealthy businessmen in Devakottai requested the supreme scholar, Sri Meenakshi Sundaram Pillai, to compose the *sthalapurana* of the temple in a village called Kandadevi. For this, along with Subbu Oduvar[1], his disciples and staff, he undertook a journey from Tiruvavaduthurai. When they had crossed Pattukottai, the sun had set and they had not yet found a place to spend the night. After about 9 pm, they came to a small village. They asked the villagers for a place to cook their meal and were directed to the *agraharam* in the village. When they reached the area, there was just one house—a very small hut with a thatched roof. On Pillai's instructions, one of the staff went up to the house to check if there was an area for preparing food in the vicinity. There were no menfolk there at that time of the night.

A young woman, seated outside with her children, was waiting for her husband's return. She was startled by the sight of so many men. "There is no facility here," she said, and abruptly shut the door.

1 Those who recite the Tevaram hymns in Shiva temples and *mathas*.

The bullock carts were parked in the open area and some of the staff explored the region. They soon found a pond close by and completed their evening rituals. The sky was awash with moonlight. The *mahavidwan*, great scholar, returned to the carts and prepared to rest for the night, hungry and sad that he could not feed his own staff after such an arduous journey. Others followed suit and some sat down to chat and spend the night hours.

After some time, the man of the household appeared, carrying a bundle of provisions on his head. He hurried to the door and knocked. The disciples then hailed him. Presumably, seeing the number of people, he was worried about how he could feed so many at this late hour.

He gave the basket to his wife indoors and was overheard saying, "Here, take this. I must have woken and seen a good person this morning because I earned something at the places I visited! All of this is the benevolence of the Goddess. At least for two days, we don't need to fret about food."

He finished his evening rituals, and ate the morning's rice soaked in water. He then rested on a cot made of palm leaf matting, in the central courtyard of his house. Delighted that he had food stored for two days, he began to sing a verse from the *Soundaryalahari*.

"Oh, Mother who creates a life of love to the Lord of Kailasa.

How will those who do not dwell and bow thinking of

Your body that is lustrous like the autumn moon

Your plaited locks bearing the crescent moon

Your hands that always grant protection and boons,

and hold the spatika garland manifesting wisdom and grace, and books;

ever be able to compose torrents of verses sweeter than

the best honey, milk and purest of fruits?"

The meaning of this verse is: those who meditate on Ambika in this form can compose sweet verses. He sang other verses as well. Pillai's disciples heard this and concluded that he was a Tamil poet. They identified the songs he was singing. When Pillai heard this, he expressed a desire to meet this poet and listen to his verses again.

When they knocked on the door, the Brahmin was scared that they might compel him to feed all of them, and said, "I have been travelling the whole day and only now have returned and eaten what little I've got. I can't come out now."

The students assured him that he had no cause for worry.

"We are not asking for food, our master only wanted to listen to your songs. You can sing them here instead of there."

"Who is this person in the middle of this forest who wants to listen to my songs? Surely, I can oblige this request," he said, as he stepped out of the door with his cot. He placed it next to Pillai and recited his poems once more.

Pillai then asked him, "What else have you learned?"

The Brahmin replied, "I have learned how to beg. My father was a Tamil poet and what little I know is from what he taught me in childhood. I keep reciting them all the time. Though I want to read, I have no books. All my father's books were borrowed and none were returned. I cannot learn from another teacher, since I need to travel to villages and homes in search of food throughout the day. I would love to borrow books from others and read them. But who will lend me any? They may not think I am a scholar. From my ancestor's times, we have had a right to receive a share of the harvests in these places (*mahamai*). During harvest time, if I make an appeal, I get some grain. All my days are spent like this. So, I repeat what I know when I have time. I was singing today because at least this much good fortune the Goddess has blessed me with. I love Tamil. There is no one in this region who can teach me. Even if there was, no one will willingly teach me. I have to work for them the whole day after which they may teach me a few things reluctantly. With my hand-to-mouth existence, where is the time for such luxuries?

"In Mayuram, it seems there is a great Tamil scholar called Meenakshi Sundaram Pillai. I am told he is generous to the poor. Not only does the great man teach them, but he also gives them food and clothing. I am told that if one spends just a few months with him, one's knowledge will be enhanced. Is there a philanthropist like that in these times? I would very much like to be his student. However, I am married and also have many children too. Do I look after them and find food for them or enjoy my love for learning Tamil? I wish I could meet him just once, but when daily life is such a toil, it is impossible. You know, my life is like that proverb: for every handspan I climb, I slip down by a cubit. What can I do? I can't see him even once. My plight is not worth speaking of." And he went on and on in this vein.

As he continued, a student gently tapped him and whispered into his ears, "The person reclining here is the same Pillai that you spoke of. He is on his way to expound the Kandadevi Puranam." The poor Brahmin poet immediately sprang from his cot, speechless with joy.

He exclaimed, "How fortunate I am! This land has indeed been really blessed!" He was transfixed. "Let me come back in a minute," he said, as he ran back indoors.

Presumably, he was going to search for provisions and to cook a meal for everyone. The others were amazed at his love and respect. "We must not trouble him. Where will this pauper go? Where will he get the provisions in a small village, at this time?" A few students restrained him and calmed him down.

They assured him that they had all the provisions and vessels needed and gave them to him. He and his wife soon prepared a meal for Pillai and his students. After the meal, instead of sleeping, in his excitement, he spent all night clarifying his many doubts about Tamil literature. As Pillai began to leave for his journey, in the morning, the person beseeched him to enjoy his hospitality. After the morning meal, Pillai and his students prepared to depart. Seeing the poet's streaming eyes, Pillai said that he was happy to accept the poet in his entourage and gave the poet provisions and money for his family. The poet spent a few months travelling with him, before returning home.

Thereafter, every year, the poet would visit Pillai in Tiruvavaduthurai and spend a few months studying under him, looking at old books and receiving a small honorarium from the pontiff in the *matha*.

The Old Table

In November 1903, I moved from the Government Arts College in Kumbakonam to Presidency College in Chennai, succeeding the Tamil pundit Sri Vai Mu Sadagopa Ramanujachariar. Mr J.P. Bilderbeck was the college principal. He was a learned man and had known me from my Kumbakonam days (since he was there too), and liked me very much.

I first called on him and he was courteous and polite to me. He asked me to take charge from the current teacher and told me that should I need anything, I could approach him. I went to the Tamil department and took charge.

There was an old table and chair for the Tamil pundit, but there was no platform.

When I was in Kumbakonam, there was no separate room for the Tamil class. For every other subject, there was a separate room, which the teachers entered to take their classes. Each of them had a platform made of wooden planks with a chair and table on it. Having taught in classrooms like this, I thought a city like Chennai would have better facilities, but the reality was different from my expectations. Because the table was on the floor, I was not able to see the faces of the students. Once locked, it was difficult to unlock. Once unlocked, it was difficult to lock. The surface was split in many places and you could see what was inside. There was a provision on one side to store a slate and stylus, and on the other side, pen and ink bottle. Clearly it was an ancient table!

This table must be one of the items in existence from the founding days of the college. As for the chair! It matched the table in age.

I was well aware of the great Tamil scholars who had served as Tamil pundits for the 100 years of the college. Tandavaraya Mudaliar, who wrote the *Panchatantra Vasanam*; Sivakozhundu Desikar, who published the *Tiruvasagam*; Mahalingam Iyer, the grammarian; the poet, Visakaperumal Iyer; Purasapakkam Ponnambalam Mudaliar; Srinivasaraghavachariar; Rajagopala Pillai and other great scholars, who were all Tamil pundits from the days when this 'college' was just a high school. I was very proud that I was in the place they had once occupied, and had not expected to use the same table and chair they had used. I was reminded of them every time I looked at the table and chair. The patience of these great scholars and the indifference of the authorities were the reasons behind these old objects being permanent fixtures in this room. I consoled myself by saying, "Even if the furniture is uncomfortable and impractical, at least it reminds me of a great legacy." What else could I do?

That day, during his daily rounds, the principal stopped by my class and asked me if everything was all right. I replied, "There is no complaint about the comfort. Here, look at this table; it is impossible to see a another like this. It is a witness to the century-old history of the college. It tells us how the old teachers used slates and stylus. Each dent speaks of their lives, and fortunately, because, I know the great contributions they all made and it reminds me of them. The chair is a worthy companion to the table. My only grievance is that I alone enjoy the heritage of these pieces. They both deserve to be in a museum, but I am lucky to have them here instead."

The principal had a hearty laugh.

"Experts say teachers should be on the same level with students; and we can follow this here. Since without a platform, the teacher and students are at the same level. Anyway, why should a teacher see the faces of the students? Only his voice has to travel to their ears!"

The principal left laughing.

After lunch when I returned, I was stunned. My room had been transformed into a stage setting. I wondered whether I had strayed into the wrong room.

The floor was covered with a mat (as I had imagined it would be before I arrived), there was a wooden platform and over it, a beautiful table and two chairs! I could even sit and chat with a visitor. In the corner was a beautiful cupboard to store my books.

Is this not how a leader should be? To know what his teachers need and arrange it quickly and efficiently is indeed praiseworthy! I was overjoyed and immediately made my way to his room to thank him.

The old table was still in a corner of my room as desired by me. I had the lock repaired and used that as well. I delighted in explaining the significance of the table to visitors.

Some years later, there was a new Principal called J.S. Stone. He had also taught in Kumbakonam and knew of me. During his time (in 1908), I had taken a week off to travel out of Chennai. At that time, he had asked for a new platform, table and chair for a new English teacher. In their hurry, the concerned department gave mine away to the new teacher and placed my old table on a small platform. The new platform was very narrow with space only for the table and chair. There was no space in front or at the rear or in the sides. If one sat on the chair in a hurry, it was even liable to fall over.

When I returned, I saw the table and chair and a smaller platform. Previously, a new table had replaced my old table. Now, another old table had replaced that table. I was very disappointed and consoled myself by saying that perhaps the room did not like new tables, chairs and a larger platform. I waited for an opportune moment to bring this to the notice of the Principal.

Fortunately, that afternoon, the Principal walked past my room. Normally I would be taking class. That day, as soon as I saw him, I rose and went out to meet him. Noting my changed manner, "Is everything all right?" he asked.

"Everything is fine, but there is something I need to mention."

"Please tell me," said the Principal.

"It is not a big matter, the table and other bits of furniture that have been here for such a long time, have been replaced. This table is old, but that is of no consequence. The platform is the one that bothers me. When I teach, looking at the students, I am thinking only of the chair. The platform is very narrow. While teaching, in my excitement should I move, then so will the chair, and both will fall to the floor. So, I am always teaching with this fear in my heart."

As he listened to me, Stone smiled. He was also angry with the persons who had done this, but left without saying anything.

The next day, my table, chairs and platform were back in my room.

The Wondrous Act of Catching a Thief[1]

When I was working in the Government Arts College, Kumbakonam, I spent time with all my colleagues and we enjoyed our chats. Each one had a special quality that I appreciated. Some of them I liked and respected very much. R.V. Srinivasa Iyer was one such person.

He had a sharp intellect, an insatiable love of learning, was straightforward and by nature, helpful. If he set his mind to it, he would accomplish things others could not. Since he was very good in mathematics, he was called "Euclid" Srinivasa Iyer. If any teacher was absent, he would step in and handle their class with ease.

He did not think: "This is my area and that is someone else's." There are some people who would put themselves and others into grief by magnifying small mistakes into big ones. He was not one of them. His magnanimous nature did not give room for nitpicking. People who knew him would want to be his friend forever. Unlike most, who save something for future exigencies, he would always give and share to a fault.

1 Originally published in *Ananda Vikatan*, Deepavali issue, 1938.

He taught at Kumbakonam Arts College and then in Chennai, at Presidency College. He then joined the Revenue Board and eventually headed the Registration Office. He was well respected in all his positions.

About fifty years back, he used to live in a rented house in Mylapore South Mada Street on the western side. He was always entertaining guests. Once, his guest was a teacher who was a classmate and former colleague from his Kumbakonam days.

In those days, the Mada streets in Mylapore were not as crowded as they are today. There were many thieves, burglaries were common, and every day, this teacher heard stories of vessels and clothes going missing, and wondered why with so many people around, the thieves weren't apprehended. He assumed that the residents were not brave enough to catch and punish the thieves. Now this guest was both courageous and strong.

One day, as someone was sharing the story of a recent burglary and others were sympathising, this teacher grew very angry and retorted, "These people call themselves men, but don't have the courage to catch a few thieves!"

He gnashed his teeth as he said this. His fist involuntarily clenched, and he twirled his moustache and imagined himself capturing a thief, and then he told himself how he would deal with one and voiced his challenge.

Srinivasa Iyer had, on his terrace, erected a thatched roof for his overnight guests to sleep. One part of that had a thatched wall partition with fine sand spread on the floor for his guests to use as a toilet.

The teacher from Kumbakonam also slept there. One night he lay sleepless thinking about the stories about thieves and his own plan to capture them and show his valour. At about midnight, he heard a sound. Someone was walking noiselessly, outside the partition. “Today is my day! Let me teach this thief a lesson he will never forget!” said the teacher. He observed the shadow cautiously and even stopped breathing. He quivered in excitement, started perspiring, and his hands were eager to capture the thief.

The man slowly walked towards the thatched partition. The brave hero quietly left his cot and pursued him. The man went inside the thatched partition and squatted to relieve himself. In a flash, the teacher pounced on his back and caught him tightly.

The man mumbled, but the teacher had a tight grip, and shouted, “Hey thief, you are well and truly caught! Do you think you could escape me like you have in the past? Your gang knows these lily-livered creatures are incapable of catching thieves and that is why you have been carrying on your exploits undeterred. You are well and truly caught today.”

The teacher was deaf to the words of the person he was gripping.

In all this commotion, those sleeping upstairs woke up, others from downstairs hurried up the stairs with lamps. “Look! Tie him up! I have been waiting all these days and have caught him today!" he said proudly. Those who held lamps, cast the light on the captive and everyone began to laugh, much to the puzzlement of the teacher. The more he asked, the more heartily everyone laughed, and finally the host, Srinivasa Iyer, came to the scene.

"This man is our cook. Is *he* the thief you caught?" asked one person.

"I asked him to sleep here, just in case one of you needed some help. Did you catch my cook thinking he is a thief?" asked Srinivasa Iyer.

"Everyone had finished their dinner. My master had asked me to get meals cooked earlier than usual tomorrow. So, after cleaning everything, I kept aside the provisions for tomorrow and prepared the vegetables. All this took till midnight. I then came upstairs and went to that side of the partition. After that, someone pounced on me and held me tightly. I was petrified it was a thief or the spirit in the nearby banyan tree." This added to the laughter. There was a banyan tree close to the house, and the local women and many others were afraid that it was haunted.

What could the brave hero do? Poor man, he quietly went back to sleep. From then on, if someone spoke about thieves in front of him, he would slip away silently.

The Richness of Tamil[1]

There are many Shaivite *mathas* in Tamil Nadu. They have been flourishing from ancient times. Some of them own landed properties and branch *mathas* too. These lands and wealth were acquired by the greatness of the pontiffs who headed the *mathas* at crucial times, and the efforts of the ascetics who had taken their advice.

The *thambirans* captivated their disciples from many parts of Tamil Nadu by their wisdom. In return, their devotees gave them many gifts. The *thambirans* selflessly surrendered all the wealth at the feet of the heads of the mathas which thus, became prosperous.

The Tamil world knows the Tiruvavaduthurai Adheenam. The *thambirans* who served this *matha*, received lands like this and gave them to the Adheenam. Sri Shivajnanayogi and Sri Kachiyappa Swami gave lands they received in Chennai and Kanchipuram to their spiritual teachers.

Around 200 years ago, there was a *thambiran* like this in Tiruvavaduthurai Adheenam. Neither his name nor the

1 From the collection, *Kandadhum Kettadhum, Pudhiyadhum Pazhaiyadhum*, 9th edition 2014. U.Ve. Sa Library publication.

name of the head of the Adheenam at that time are known today. That Thambiran was a Tamil scholar, who could sing sweet verses with great imagination. He was also learned in Sanskrit and music. His devotion to his spiritual teacher was unparalleled. He was intent on improving that particular Adheenam. He was a Shiva puja expert, and his radiant appearance and purity born of impeccable asceticism enhanced his greatness. On account of his deep devotion to the Adheenam and his desire that the Shiva puja and Maheswara puja at the Adheenam be special, he went to many places and, by his congeniality, made friends with the zamindars and wealthy men, received what they generously donated to him and brought it to the Adheenam. Wherever he went, he captivated all by his learning and poetic excellence. His radiance attracted even the unlearned ones. People who learnt that the Tiruvavaduthurai Adheenam was a place where Shaivism flourished, became more devoted to it.

"If this sage looks like Shiva's attendant himself, Tiruvavaduthurai, where there is a *gnanadesikar*, a teacher of others like him, must indeed be Kailasam on earth," people thought to themselves. Many went to Tiruvavaduthurai and had a darshan of the *gnanadesikar*, rejoiced in it and shared their ecstasy with others when they returned. Thus, the endeavours of that Thambiran bore good results.

He heard that the then ruler of Thiruvananthapuram had great regard for scholars and would shower largesse on them. So, he went to Thiruvananthapuram to meet that king. Some of the wealthy Shaivaites who were there, heard about his coming and welcomed him. From them, the Thambiran learnt that the king was only interested in Sanskrit and music, and that he rarely gave audience to Tamil scholars. However, he resolved that he would somehow, with Shiva's grace try to meet him. He wondered how, but he was told that it was not likely to happen. He remained in Thiruvananthapuram for a while. The Shaivites took care of him with great respect. One day the king decided to have the darshan of the family deity Sri Padmanabhaswami. Having heard of this, the Thambiran became determined to meet him somehow, and waited for him on the path to the temple with gifts. The guards who led the way saw the Thambiran standing on the path. They were filled with awe when they saw him standing with sacred ash on his forehead and body, glowing ear ornaments and the rudraksha garland with the traditional Gowrishankar pendant (carrying images of Shiva and Parvathi), his tall coiffure of matted hair, the long beard with moustache and the deep ochre robe. They were afraid to remove him from the path like they would others who stood in the way.

The king saw the Thambiran, and was struck by his radiant appearance. The Thambiran thought this was the opportune moment and respectfully offered to him the gifts he had brought. Taken aback by this unexpected act, the king asked the persons standing near him, who this person was. At that juncture, Thambiran sang a poem set to seven-line metre with specific restrictions.

"Oh, King of Vanji with the spear that roams among the crowd of foes! I am the woman Senthamizh, I rejoiced in being worshipped by all the three Chera, Chola and Pandya kings. Of them, one of your ancestors, Cheraman Perumal Nayanar, decorated me before Lord Shiva with the matted locks and the moon on his head. Now you do not respect me who had such greatness and was cherished by your people, because you are afraid that Aariyam (Sanskrit) a common woman will get offended. So, I will go away to Pothigai *malai*[2] belonging to the sage, Agastya."

The verse was composed keeping in mind the practice of a woman going to her natal home, when she has been abandoned by her husband who has developed a relationship with another woman. The verbal comparison of Sanskrit to a common woman may appear offensive, but the meaning really is that Sanskrit is common to all the regions in India. This revealed the poetic skill of the Thambiran. After informing the king that he had been waiting for many days for this audience, he explained the meaning of the verse to the king by using Sanskrit terms. The king on grasping the meaning was impressed by the intelligence of the Thambiran. He also realized that it was a mistake to have ignored Tamil. After directing his subordinates to give Thambiran whatever he wanted, the king proceeded to the temple to have darshan. After the darshan, he returned to the palace and, on completing his appointed tasks, he sent for the Thambiran.

The Thambiran met the king. After the conversation the king not only learnt about the richness of Tamil, but also how the Chera kings had nurtured the language.

2 Podhigai Hills/Mountains.

Then the Thambiran told the king about the greatness of Tiruvavaduthurai Adheenam. The king realized the clarity and sharpness of his intellect and his respect for the Adheenam grew. The king learnt that any assistance given to the Adheenam would be utilized for Shiva *puja*, Maheswara *puja* and other charitable projects, and that any development of the Adheenam would benefit the whole world just as a water body filled to the brim will benefit everyone. Thambiran enjoyed the king's hospitality for some time and explained the greatness of Tamil to the best of his ability.

Then the Thambiran, desirous to return to Tiruvavaduthurai, wanted to take leave of the king. The king was reluctant to let him go, as he had never known such a person and was also impressed by the Thambiran's goodness. He gave him plenty of gifts, silks, shawls, puja vessels made of silver and other things. He gave him a palanquin and also the wages for the palanquin bearers. He told the Thambiran, "Please visit again."

Thambiran returned to Tiruvavaduthurai and placed at the feet of the guru all that he had received. He narrated all that had transpired in Thiruvananthapuram and said, "This is the wealth earned by Tamil."

Though that Thambiran and the king of Thiruvananthapuram have left their mortal coils, the wealth brought by Tamil belongs to Tiruvavaduthurai even today. (This anecdote was shared by Trichy C. Thyagaraja Chettiar.)

Devotion to the Teacher[1]

One of the disciples of Trichy Meenakshi Sundaram Pillai was Sundaram Pillai, who was deeply devoted to him. If he came to know that his teacher had some problem or difficulty, he would somehow try to solve it. If someone spoke of him in a less than respectful manner, he would challenge that person and make them feel sorry. He was worldly wise, extremely articulate, and had the maturity and wisdom to decide how to act. He had many friends. His virtues were such that his friends would somehow do Sundaram Pillai's bidding.

Once, Meenakshi Sundaram Pillai, obtained the Tiruthanigai Puranam, the Purana about the sacred town Tiruttani, from Kanchipuram Sabapathi Mudaliar who was in Chennai, and began to learn it on his own, analyzing it deeply. He could not fully understand some portions of *Agathiyan Arul Peru Padalam* (where the sage Agastya is blessed). He approached many people to find out the meaning, but he was not successful. Then someone told him that he could divine the meaning with the help of a work called

1 From the collection, *Kandadhum Kettadhum, Pudhiyadhum Pazhaiyadhum*, 9th edition 2014. U.Ve. Sa Library publication.

Shivadarumottiram, which he immediately tried to locate, but unsuccessfully. Then he learnt that the book was available with an Abhishekasthar Desikar (a Shaivaite guru) in Trichy. Meenakshi Sundaram Pillai told him that if it were loaned to him for a while, he would study it and return it. Though he made the request repeatedly, the guru did not relent. So, he apprehended others to make the request on his behalf. His efforts failed repeatedly. Every time the guru gave a different reason for not acceding to the request; that it was placed with the puja and could be removed; that the world did not know its greatness; that the meaning could not be discerned easily and so on. Repeated requests only hardened the guru's stance. Then Pillai thought that he might agree if he were offered some money. So, he said he would make a payment as security for taking the book on loan. The guru refused even that offer. Pillai was saddened that all his efforts had failed.

"I searched everywhere for this book. Even though it is right here I am unable to get it. Will not the stubborn heart melt?"

One day, Sundaram Pillai saw his teacher looking crestfallen. He approached his teacher respectfully and asked him the reason. Meenakshi Sundaram Pillai narrated the whole story of how he could not understand the meaning of *Agathiyan Arul Peru Padalam* when he was reading Tiruthanigai Puranam, how he heard that it could be found in *Shivadarumottiram*, how he learnt that the Abhishekasthar in that town was in possession of the book and how he had tried several times and failed to borrow it.

Sundaram Pillai told him that if it was true that the said person had the book, it could be obtained and that his guru (Meenakshi Sundaram Pillai) need not worry on that count. The teacher wondered how Sundaram Pillai could succeed when he had failed even after several attempts.

One day, a rich man landed at the aforesaid Desikar's house in a two-horse drawn chariot. An employee ran to the Desikar's house and stood at the front hall and asked gently if it was the Desikar's house.

"Yes, it is. Who are you? Why do you want him?" A person from inside the house enquired.

"Is Desikar in? I can only tell *him* the purpose of this call."

"I am he. Tell me what you want to say."

As this conversation was in progress, another employee came and spread a rich carpet on the front *pial*. Yet another placed a bolster pillow against the wall. The rich man came sat on the *pial* so decorated with a majestic air. Suitably liveried men walked up and stood before him respectfully, their hands covering their mouths. When he saw them, the employee who was conversing from indoors, rushed out.

Desikar who had come to the front hall, saw what had taken place at the entrance to his house.

"Somebody important has come with all paraphernalia, perhaps to meet me or someone else I don't know. It will soon be known. It does not befit my standing to go before that worthy personage on my own. I will go if invited." So thinking, Desikar went inside and sat on a plank picking up a book to read.

As this was happening, the employee who had been earlier talking to him went inside again slowly. He stood silently indicating that he was apprehensive about whether to call Desikar or not. Then he cleared his throat.

"Why are you here?" Desikar asked.

"My master asked me to find out if it was convenient for him to meet you."

"He may come in." Desikar got up hastily.

"My master is observing the mourning period so he will not come in."

"Oh, then I will come out and meet him. Nothing wrong if he comes in either." So saying, he stepped out wearing the *rudraksha* bead necklace and other ornaments to meet the rich man. The visitor bowed to Desikar and asked him to remain where he was. Desikar continued to gaze at the visitor. One of the visitor's staff, positioned himself by Desikar.

"Who is your master? From where has he come?" Desikar asked in a low voice.

"My master belongs to a big zamindar family from the south. He came with his mother to have darshan at Chidambaram. He halted here in Tiruchirappalli, to have darshan of the temples of Jambunatha, Thayumanavar and Ranganathar. He stayed in a bungalow in the cantonment, intending to remain here for at least three days. His mother fell ill. In spite of all efforts and a lot of expense, she attained Shiva's abode last evening. The cremation was done at once. If she had passed away in our native place, the ceremonies would have been done very elaborately. But what to do? It is all

God's will, not ours. The ritual gathering of the bones was also done today. When we were enquiring who is the best person to contact for certain matters, they mentioned your name. So, my master has come to you. Though we are willing to pay the cost, nothing is available here as they are at our place. Even the persons who perform the ceremonies are not available so easily here. We tried as much as we could yesterday, so we are leaving today to our place to perform the concluding rites."

"Everything is available here. What can you not get, if you have money? I know everyone here, carpenters, goldsmiths, vessel merchants and textile shops. There are suitable places to do the obsequies. If I were rich, I could accomplish anything. Please do not hesitate, you can do everything here. Let your master do the rites here itself."

"My master is not hesitating about expenditure," the employee replied, on hearing the persuasive words of Desikar, "We have enough people to buy all the materials also. But my master has one wish. It seems there is a book called *Shivadarumottiram*. His desire is to read that during this mourning period. It seems on the advice of some elders he secured this book when his father passed away and he was reading it at that time. It is not suitable if it is in Grantha script. My master wants it in Tamil and for this purpose he wants to go back to his native place." After saying this the employee said in a soft tone to Desikar, "He is not listening to us though we have told him several times that we should complete the rites here itself. What does it matter if he does not read that book?"

"*Shivadarumottiram* in Tamil is with me. If you want you may use it. What is the purpose of my having it if it cannot be of help to noble people like you?" Desikar said looking at the rich nobleman.

The employee who was standing, aware of his master's intention, requested Desikar to write down in detail all that was required for the performance of the obsequies. Desikar brought writing materials and dictated a detailed note. On looking at it, one of the members of the entourage said that it would cost much more in their native place.

"Even this expenditure no one is prepared to incur in this place," Desikar said.

"I request you not only to purchase all that is necessary but also to be with me during the performance of the entire rites". The rich man told Desikar very respectfully and got into the carriage, to leave.

"When should we come next?" asked the employee who stood nearby.

"It is enough if you come one week before the final rites. Everything can be purchased on credit."

Having said so, Desikar, rushed inside requesting the rich man to wait for a minute. He then fetched the copy of *Shivadarumottiram* and handed it over.

"Please excuse me for not giving this book sooner. Acquaintance with people like you is more important for me than this book. What advice can I give to people like you, who are famous for helping others in need," Desikar said, gripping the carriage.

The rich man said that he understood everything and nothing more was needed to be said and gave him five rupees. The carriage dashed away. The attendants ran in front and behind the carriage. Desikar looked at this sight with delight and went back to his house.

Out of the blue, one day, Sundaram Pillai came to his teacher and handed over a book saying, "Here is *Shivadarumottiram.*"

"Where did you get this, *appa*?" Asked Meenakshi Sundaram Pillai, after glancing at the book and looked at him.

"What happened in your house? Why have you removed your moustache? I have not heard of your bereavement. Why did you not inform me?" he asked Sundaram Pillai.

"I will answer you later. It is better if a copy of the whole work is prepared within one week and returned to me. No one should know that a copy has been made."

Meenakshi Sundaram Pillai agreed to do accordingly and distributed the manuscript amongst his students and friends giving them ten leaves each and to copy down. He himself copied down the remaining leaves. The work was thus copied in seven days. On the eighth day, the palm leaf manuscript was returned to Sundaram Pillai. Thereafter, he read the book and cleared his doubts in the Thanigai Puranam.

Sundaram Pillai called his friend who had played the role of one of the rich man's employees, handed over the *Shivadarumottiram* manuscript and a gold coin and asked him to give it all to Desikar. On seeing this person, Desikar was delighted and welcomed him heartily. The person in the employee's disguise gave him the gold coin and the manuscript.

"All my masters' relatives insisted that he should complete the obsequies only in his native place. Therefore, my master has left with all the people who were accompanying him. He regretted that he was unable to personally take leave of you. I am confident that he will soon invite you to his place," saying which, he left. Desikar was a bit disappointed that he was appeased by the gift of the gold coin. Later, Meenakshi Sundaram Pillai learnt about all this through someone else and was filled with amazement. His heart was filled with joy at the love his student Sundaram Pillai had for him.

Sundaram Pillai did not go and see his teacher for a number of days because he was afraid of what Meenakshi Sundaram Pillai would think of the trick that he had played. Meenakshi Sundaram Pillai immediately asked him to meet him. Sundaram Pillai reached his teacher.

"What is this, *appa*? Can you do something like this?"

In response, he recited the *Kural* which laid down that when a falsehood would bring only good results without any harm, then that falsehood takes the place of truth. (*Poymaiyum 30.292 Tirukural*).

"I only followed this *Tirukural*. No one was harmed by what I did. If Ayya thinks it is wrong, please forgive me".

I have heard Meenakshi Sundaram Pillai narrate this several times and praise Sundaram Pillai's devotion to his teacher and his quick wittedness.

Appa Dikshitar's Discomfiture

In Tiruvavaduthurai *matha*, Meenakshi Sundaram Pillai taught several Tamil texts to many students. When Subramania Desikar was the Adheenam head, Pillai began taking Tirunagaikkarona Puranam, the Purana of the sacred town of Nagapattinam or Nagaikkaronam in the presence of the pontiff. When they had reached the description of the deluge in the 'Talaviseda Padalam' (the chapter describing the special features of the place) a person called Appa Dikshitar came from Tiruvalangadu. He belonged to the family of the great Sanskrit scholar Appayya Dikshitar. Appa Dikshitar was well-versed in Sanskrit grammar and Shaiva literature. He had many students who had studied under him with the aid of the Tiruvavaduthurai *matha*, and had become great teachers themselves.

Dikshitar stood and listened to the students reading aloud that particular portion. As he did this, for some reason, he kept contradicting the content of each verse. Pillai replied and also explained. Without appreciating this, Dikshitar continued in the same vein. These interruptions upset Meenakshi Sundaram Pillai.

Subramania Desikar observed Pilllai's discomfiture at how the lessons were being interrupted. He spoke to the Dikshitar, discussed the purpose of his visit after which the Dikshitar took leave. Desikar indicated that the lessons must continue. The classes went on as usual. At the end of the class, Pillai said that if Tiruvalangattu Thyagaraja Sastrigal had been present, he would have rejoiced and that it was a pity he was not there.

Thyagaraja Sastrigal also belonged to the Appayya Dikshitar lineage. He was learned in many shastras and in the study of the Vedas. He was an expert in the *Alankara Shastra*. He was a poet, and a musician and could play the veena. He was a linguist and knew many languages including English. He had been employed in Pudukkottai for a while. He was a good orator and his lectures were well appreciated. He was a narrator of *Shivakathai* too. Even in casual conversation, he could captivate his listeners. When Subramania Desikar became the junior pontiff, it was Sastrigal who taught him in his leisure hours, many Sanskrit works explaining clearly and crisply literary nuances and special features. It was he who enhanced Desikar's stature in the eyes of the world and, in particular, it could be said that he was *the* Sanskrit teacher. He also had a deep regard for Pillai.

The day after Appa Dikshitar left, Sastrigal came to Tiruvavaduthurai with his students. He had gone to Tiruvalangadu from Pudukkottai and from there he had come to see the pontiff of the Adheenam.

Desikar welcomed him joyfully even as he entered and they sat conversing for some time. Meenakshi Sundaram Pillai also joined them.

"Please tell Sastrigal what you taught yesterday." Desikar told Pillai.

And Pillai explained four or five verses that he had taught the previous day. Sastrigal was in raptures; he extolled Pillai.

"There is no one to match you in such compositions, your imaginative skill is unmatched. I am not so conversant in Tamil poetry, but even I can understand the beauty of these verses. This is what is called poetic excellence. You must have been Kamban in your previous birth."

"Do you see any mistakes in these verses?" asked Desikar.

"There cannot be any mistakes even in the locations where these verses are recited. So, how can there be any mistakes in them. They embody perfection."

"If someone pointed out some fault, what will you say?"

"I will say that he is a rogue, a villain, an ignoramus and arrogant. Which fellow said so?"

"It was your *guru*."

"Is that so?" Sastrigal stood up at once, trembling. He lifted his hands over his head in obeisance and turned in the direction of Tiruvalangadu closing his eyes in reverence.

"Haraharamahadeva! Shiva Shiva! Forgive my words uttered in haste. Oh! My Acharya!"

He raised his eyes upwards and stood in meditation.

Desikar smiled.

"Sastrigal, calm down. We never expected that you would take it so much to heart. We had to say it because that is what happened. Please forgive what happened. It was our wish to seek your appreciation of those verses and that is why it happened this way."

"Sannidhanam should not have placed me in such an embarrassing situation. I am perplexed. Please let me not be dragged into such a position again."

It was already late, so the visitors took leave. The students who were disheartened by the events of the previous day, felt greatly comforted by Sastrigal's praise.

The Scribe Whose Pride Was Quelled

When the *mahavidwan* Sri Meenakshi Sundaram Pillai composed the Tirunagaik Karona Puranam, the scribe was Muthambalpuram (Orathanadu) Gopala Pillai. Before Gopala Pillai joined as the great poet's student, he had been a student of Narayanaswami Vadyar, a famous poet, who was a teacher at the Tamil College of Muthambalpuram. Gopala Pillai was very intelligent, and very good at writing on palm leaves. He was of the opinion that he was an expert scribe.

Once when Sri Meenakshi Sundaram Pillai was resting, Vaidyalingam Pillai, who took care of the house and was devoted to him, told the students that Gopala Pillai was an expert scribe. To which, Gopala Pillai replied, "True, but *Ayya* does not dictate till my hand hurts." Though he spoke softly, Pillai, who was resting, heard this. He thought if he came out at once, Gopala Pillai would be afraid and embarrassed, so he remained in his room for some more time and then came out. Lessons and dictation continued as usual.

One day, after completing his daily rituals, Pillai sat in his easy chair. Gopala Pillai got ready with the palm leaves and the stylus. Other students and friends, seated at their respective places, listened to the verses as they were composed. The great poet asked them to read the portion in the Purana from where he had to start the dictation. But he did not begin at once, he thought deeply for a while, inhaled some snuff, wiped his hands and then began.

Pillai did not use snuff often. But if he did before dictation, words would flow without pause. Then the people around him would deduce that verses would now be composed swiftly.

He began dictating and went on without a pause. That day's class was about *Sundaravidanga Padalam* of the Purana, full of imagery. The scribe kept writing unceasingly. It started at 7 in the morning. Usually, Pillai would dictate till 10 and then go in for his bath and *puja*. Since he kept dictating at a rapid pace, the scribe's hand began to hurt. He longed for it to strike 10 o'clock. Even after it turned 10, the *mahavidwan* did not stop, and continued to dictate.

The *thavasi pillai*, cook, arrived and indicated that it was time for his bath. The *mahavidwan* nodded, but did not get up, and continued dictating. It turned 11, but the dictation continued. Gopala Pillai's little finger on the right hand and the right thumb grew stiff and blood shot, and the pain was intense. He could not bear it. He thought that if he indicated his pain, the dictation would stop, and he stroked the left hand with his right, and right hand with his left after putting down the writing materials. But the poet did not seem to notice and continued to dictate the verses. It was 11:30. Gopala Pillai felt ashamed to speak of his pain, ground his teeth and continued. Most of the students had left at 11. The great poet did not stop. At 12, Gopala Pillai realized he could not write another single word. When Pillai paused a little to think, Gopala Pillai tied the palm leaves with a string and placed the stylus in its case. He then stood up suddenly and prostrated himself before his teacher, Meenakshi Sundaram Pillai, and did not get up.

"What happened? Why are you doing this? What is the matter? Get up."

"I cannot write another word. My pride that I am a matchless scribe has been quelled today forever. Further, I have realized your greatness truly only today. Whose incarnation you are I do not know, nor whose greatness is reflected in you. I have never seen, nor heard anyone with this felicity to compose verses. Today's lesson was not a simple one, if someone else attempted to deal with this, they would have taken many days. But you did it effortlessly and with such speed! I feel it will take me many days to resume this task. I must be forgiven for halting my work midway."

"*Appa*, if you had only told me of your pain, I would have stopped earlier. Because this is a very special portion, I did not have the heart to halt, for I feared what I had mentally composed I might forget. That is why I went on. You go for your bath."

Then he too left to have his bath. People in Mayavaram and surrounding places got to know of what happened. All of them were filled with admiration at Pillai's greatness and praised him in person.

Gopala Pillai went around with a very sad face. Vaidyalingam Pillai came in the afternoon and asked him why he looked depressed. He had heard what had happened from others.

"What? At last, your pride tumbled down! You said that day that ayya has never dictated till your hand hurt. It upset me very much then. The frisky bull will have to bear the heaviest burden."

Meenakshi Sundaram Pillai came in exactly at this point.

"Don't say anything about him. He is a good boy. He will feel hurt." And he stopped Vaidyalingam Pillai from saying anything more. It took many days for Gopala Pillai's hand to heal.

Gopala Pillai who had always respected his teacher, was now filled with great admiration. He thought Pillai was really a divine incarnation and treated him with great reverence.

The Sculpture at Venganoor Temple[1]

No one in Tamil Nadu will be unaware of Sivaprakasa Swamingal, from Turaimangalam, who was renowned as a storehouse of imagination and an emperor among poets. Venganoor, commonly known as Tiruvengai is one of those sacred places which remain in the memory of Tamils because of Swamigal's poetic garlands. Sivaprakasa Swamigal has composed several works on this place, a *kovai*[2] celebrated by poets as a *mandirikkovai*, an *ula*, a *kalambakam* and an *alankaram*. This Venganoor is situated in Perumpuliyur taluk in the Trichy area.

The sculptures in this temple are matchless. They have been praised in *Tiruvengaikkovai* and *Tiruvengai Ula*. The words can roughly be translated as Tiruvengai which has no equal—the temple built by the righteous Annamalai and is a poem in stone. This is the story about the place.

Lingappa Reddiar of Turaimangalam belonged to a traditionally rich family. His family name was Vallakol.

1 From the collection, *Kandadhum Kettadhum, Pudhiyadhum Pazhaiyadhum*, 9th edition 2014. U.Ve. Sa Library publication.

2 Genre of Tamil poetry, usually telling a story.

He had two sons Annamalai and Neelakantan. It was Annamalai Reddiar who built the Tiruvengaikoil.

He was a virtuous, learned man devoted to Lord Shiva, well-read in Tamil literature with great regard for Tamil scholars, and respected like the ruler of a small kingdom. He had great respect for Sivaprakasa Swamigal and supported him in many ways by making available many comforts for him. The stone water tanks constructed by him are admired by people even today. That great poet who did not deign to praise mortals in his verses, actually lauded Reddiar in a poem.

He has praised Reddiar as the son of Lingayyan who was the personification of benevolence, who supported "my people," who never said no to whoever asked for some help, who took care of Tamil poets and so on. Though Swamigal was an ascetic, he used the phrase "supporter of my people" —"எம் குடிதாங்கி (*emkudithangi*)", and lavishly praised Annamalai Reddiar, who deserved nothing less.

Annamalai Reddiar lived in Venganoor which was one of the many villages he owned. It was his habit to observe austerities on every *pradosham*[3] day and to go to Vriddhachalam to have the darshan of the deities Pazhamalainathar and Periyanayaki Ammai. He unfailingly observed this routine. Once when the Vellaru was in spate, and he could not cross it for his *pradosha darshan*, he was deeply saddened. That night Pazhamalainathar appeared in his dream, indicated a specific place in Venganoor, and

3 The thirteenth day of every fortnight, sacred to the worship of Shiva.

told him to install a Shiva lingam and attendant deities and worship them.

Sivaprakasa Swamigal has described this incident in beautiful words:

> Lord Shiva desired to remain in Vengai itself. By keeping His consort on His left, the desire for the woman was addressed, when He stole all the wealth from Sundaramoorthi Nayanar at Tirumuruganpoondi, the desire for gold was taken care of, all that was left was desire for land. Shiva, in the dream, appeared in his own form and was able to get land. Unlike Vishnu who, to bestow grace on the devas, shrunk his form to a dwarf and begged Emperor Mahabali for land.

Annamalai Reddiar woke up with a start and his heart melted thinking of Lord Shiva's grace. He went to the place indicated in the dream and began preparations for building a Shiva temple. He brought a Banalingam from the river Narmada, installed it and had daily darshan.

Once there was a famine in the north, and sculptors headed towards the south with their leader. When Annamalai Reddiar heard that this group would walk through Venganoor, he decided to ask them to help him with the work for the temple. When he told them of his plan, they were very happy that this kind of help was extended to them when they were afflicted by famine. They readily agreed to do the temple work.

They began their work according to the norms fixed for such work at temples. Reddiar made all arrangements for them like food and shelter, leaving no cause for complaints. Overwhelmed by his kindness, the sculptors performed their duties correctly. Reddiar inspected the temple every day. He enquired if the sculptors needed anything, and at once took care of their needs. He realized that their leader was in the habit of chewing betel; so he engaged an *adappaikaran* who would prepare it (the *tamboolam*) for the leader. This attendant was told to give the *tamboolam* to the master sculptor, not just when he worked but also at leisure times. The master sculptor saw that the kindness extended to them was unparalleled and worked with greater zeal.

In some places, the stones laid across had to be carved on the inside, so scaffolds were put up, and the master sculptor lay on the scaffold, delicately carving the stones above him with deep concentration. The attendant stood below, regularly handing him the folded betel leaves. One day, Annamalai Reddiar came along as usual to the place where the sculptors were working. He marvelled at their extraordinary artistic skill. Very silently he came to the place where their leader was at work. He did not make any sound, as he was afraid that he might disturb him and halt the work. Since the chief sculptor was lying on his back carving the stone above, he did not notice the arrival of Reddiar. As was his practice, he stretched out his left arm for another betel roll. But at that moment, the attendant had gone out. Since Annamalai Reddiar realized that the sculptor wanted some *tamboolam*, he handed over what was given to him by his personal attendant. Totally unaware of all this, the master sculptor who was focussed on his work, slipped it into his mouth. At once he realized, it was different, because it was made of very expensive spices and fragrant ingredients. It was not the customary betel leaves and areca scrapings that he always had, so he turned to look down and saw Reddiar holding the next roll, in case the sculptor wanted another.

The master sculptor was startled. Filled with admiration and apprehension, he jumped down and fell at Reddiar's feet.

"You are blessed by birth, and an aristocrat, and you are such a great Shiva bhakta that the Lord himself appeared in your dream. Is it proper for you to do this? Your act, has made me disrespectful," he said, struggling for words.

"I have not done anything wrong. I felt you would slow down if no one handed over a *tamboolam*," replied Reddiar who was a true connoisseur.

"I did not notice your arrival. I thought it was my attendant who handed it. Its special quality and fragrance made me glance down. Should you, who are a perennial well of largesse for the needy, do this? And it was my left had I stretched!"

"You have done nothing wrong. Your hands are blessed hands. Don't I know that they are possessed of the good fortune of carving in many Shiva temples? And those sculptures will stand there for ever. No wrong was committed by my giving *tamboolam* to those hands. I did it only so that there will be no disturbance to your work."

"You gave shelter like a shady tree to us who were afflicted by famine, and we will never forget that kindness. In addition to that, what you did just now, has made me deeply indebted to you. I cannot forget you or your greatness even if I take seven births. How will I repay my gratitude? I will construct this sanctum sanctorum, with all the skill at my command and all my expertise. I must have done countless good deeds to be given the task of doing this in this place that belongs to you. The food and clothes that you have given is enough. We will not take any payment."

Then he sought permission from Reddiar and re-constructed the sanctum sculptures. Being a labour for love, and not for money, they were extraordinary. The temple was completed and the consecration was performed. The master sculptor refused payment, though Reddiar strongly insisted. But Reddiar gave expensive gifts to him and his team of sculptors, and expressed his appreciation.

This story shows how Annamalai Reddiar extended his patronage not only to poets, but to sculptors and artisans, and also showcases his extreme simplicity and informal accessible nature. To him we owe the poetry of Sivaprakasa and the sculptures in Venganoor.

Maruda Pandiyar[1]

A hundred and fifty years ago, one Maruda Servaikarar was the ruler of Shivagangai Samsthanam. On account of his greatness and goodness, his people and the scholars referred to him as Maruda Pandiyar, and actually considered him a maharaja. He donated generously to scholars, and since he himself was a Tamil scholar, he would discuss learned topics, and when he was delighted by their wisdom, he honoured them. The *prabandhams*[2] composed about him, and the verses in his praise created spontaneously are many. He was a brave warrior. It was said that robbers did not dare to enter his territory. Everyone bowed to his rule.

He was a very pious person and made arrangements for all the daily rituals to be performed in the temples under his jurisdiction. He created many religious endowments, and endowed vast extent of lands as *devadaanam* to many temples. In Kundrakkudi, which is one of the most

---

1 From the collection, *Kandadhum Kettadhum, Pudhiyadhum Pazhaiyadhum*, 9th edition 2014. U.Ve. Sa Library publication.

2 Genre of Tamil poetry, usually in praise of the divine or a patron.

important Muruga shrines, he repaired the temple tank to the south of Tiruveedhi, the road abutting the temple, and also built the steps leading to it. The tank was called Marudapuri in his honour, and some of the coconut trees that he planted around the tank stand even today. He has built some *mandapa*s on top of the Kundrakkudi hill. When they were built, many tall scaffolds were raised. The topmost one was put up by Maruda Pandiyar, and the bottom one by the zamindar Vengalappa Naicker and this was expressed by Maruda Pandyiar's people in the words "*Melaichaaram Engalappan, keezhaicharam Vengalappan.*" *Engalappan* meant our father. This indicated his people's affection for Maruda Pandyiar, and also his superior qualities.

The big tank called Yaanaimadu in Kaalaiyarkovil was also repaired by him, and he put up steps on all sides. He also built an entrance gopuram for which bricks had to be brought from afar. So, he made workers stand along the road in a line a few feet from each other, so that they could pass the bricks in a relay all the way. For all those who helped like this, he gave groundnuts, beaten rice and other things to eat and water to drink, so that they felt refreshed.

He wanted to make a big *ther*, a temple car, for the Kalaiyarkovil and he gathered all the materials and the craftsmen. But he could not get a tree big enough to be the axle. He made enquiries in various places. He heard that there was a huge maruda tree on the southern bank of the river, Vaigai, next to the temple at Thirupoovanam, which was under his jurisdiction. He sent his officials to cut it and fetch it to the site.

The officials sent their workers with the necessary implements and attempted to cut the tree. On hearing this, the priest who performed the *puja* to the main deity, an *aadishaivar* named Pushpavana Gurukkal, came rushing out.

"Don't cut the tree, don't cut the tree," he shouted and stopped them.

"Are you overruling our ruler's command?" The officials asked and urged the workers to proceed.

"In the name of the king, I bid you not to cut the tree." The priest took an oath, because he was enraged.

Hearing this, the workers stopped and reported what happened to Maruda Pandiyar who was astonished.

"When I had instructed them to cut it for the sake of Sri Kaliswarar temple, can anyone stop it? Who has the temerity? Let me check." With these thoughts running through his mind, he went with his entourage and halted at the *mandapa* near the temple for a while. The temple authorities received him with due respect, offered him the holy *vibhuti* which he applied on his forehead.

"Are the temple rituals going on routinely?" He asked the authorities. "I hear that a temple priest stopped the cutting of the tree on the banks of Vaigai. Who dared to flout my order? Is he here?"

"He was the one who gave the prasadam to your highness. He was afraid of your anger and has fled to Madurai." They said with great trepidation.

Pushpavana Gurukkal had already engaged a cart to take him to some place beyond the reach of Maruda Pandiyar's jurisdiction, because he was very apprehensive. The priest had already reached Madurai.

Maruda Pandyiar sent someone to Madurai, with an *abhayanirupam* to bring the Gurukkal back. In olden days kings sent a communication to offenders or enemies on the run assuring them that they could return without fear of any harm. This was called *abhayanirupam*. Such missives were written by rulers as a form of assurance to wrongdoers.

On seeing this letter, a relieved Pushpavana Gurukkal, though fearful, went to Thirupoovanam. Maruda Pandiyar did not want to express his anger; so he controlled himself when the Gurukkal appeared before him.

"Did you restrain the people who were sent to cut the Maruda tree?"

"Yes, your Highness."

"When I have commanded them to cut it for the Kalaiyar Kovil temple *ther*, what made you stop them?"

"There were good reasons for doing so."

The officials and townsmen who were present were afraid what the ruler would do and wondered what explanation the Gurukkal would offer.

"What are those reasons? Don't be afraid. Tell me."

"This is a celebrated and ancient temple. This is where Lord Sundareswarar of Madurai did alchemy for the sake of Ponnanaiyaal. When the bones of a dead man were thrown in to the Vaigai here, they turned into a flower. That is why it is called Pushpavanakasi. The three Shaiva saints (Sundarar, Manickavasagar and Sambandhar), reluctant to place their foot on this sacred spot, stood on the northern bank and had their darshan. To indicate this, there is a shrine for those three on the northern bank. For all these reasons this place also attracts pilgrims. Many people come daily from out of town, bathe in the Vaigai and have darshan of the deity. Vaigai does not always have much water, in summer, it dwindles to a trickle on the northern side. When people have a dip there in summer, and walk to the temple along the hot sands, they rest a little under this tree. This tree has stood here for centuries and thousands of people have taken shelter in its shade."

Maruda Pandyiar kept listening as the *gurukkal* continued giving the reasons and he realized they were all for the benefit of the public. His anger gradually subsided. He continued to listen as the gurukkal said, "I thought the royal command would not have been issued if Your Highness knew how much the people benefit from this tree. If it is cut down, pregnant women, children and the elderly who come from outside to pray at this temple, will suffer a great deal in the hot season. The people who come from the other side will also suffer. For Your Highness, there are many trees in the Samsthanam, it is not just this one tree. I am reminded of Your Highness whenever I see this tree, for it too like our Maharaja removes the affliction of the people and gladdens their hearts. Over and above all this, there is one more reason imprinted in my heart, and that is, the tree bears the name of Your Highness. For the welfare of your Highness, I do *archana* at this shrine, praying that this tree stands forever. When that is my prayer, how can I permit the tree to be cut?"

On hearing this, all those present grew very emotional. The *gurukkal* had very intelligently linked the names of the ruler and the tree, and the people were astonished and moved.

Maruda Pandyiar who had been listening without looking at the *gurukkal*'s face, now raised his head and smiled. He understood that the *gurukkal*'s motives were bonafide, and inspired by true devotion and loyalty.

"Very good, what you did was right. We appreciate your loyalty to us and the love you have for the people."

The Maruda tree was spared and so was the *gurukkal*. Another tree was used for the temple car.

(This was narrated to me by Sri Muthu Ramalinga Thevar, Zamindar of Aranmanai Siruvayal and Sri Appa Pillai who was the head clerk of Kundrakkudi Matha)

Written with a Thorn

A favour done at the right time, even if it is a small one, is more valuable than the whole world, says the *Tirukural*.

I have already written about Maruda Pandyiar, and the many stories about him passed down by word of mouth.

He was full of magnanimity; he was a Shiva devotee, a patron of scholars and a benevolent ruler.

His ancestors were not the rulers of the Samsthanam. But the ruler who preceded him was saved by him from a tiger's jaws and since he was a matchless warrior, that ruler appointed him as his successor.

It is said that there were twenty-one Tamil scholars in his *samsthanam*. To this day we can find verses in his praise written by Javvadu Pulavar, Muthuvelu Pulavar and many others. There are many villages endowed by him as *srotriyam* in favour of these learned men. The poets praised his valour and benevolence. Until a few years ago, there were elderly people in and around Shivagangai who used to share anecdotes about him.

In his later years, Maruda Pandyiar became a target for some powerful men. They tried to capture him. By his valour and intelligence, he managed to escape. Once he was staying in a *mandapa* opposite Tirukoshtiyur temple which was in his *samsthanam*. He was afflicted by a rash on his right hand. At that time, one of his confidential loyal servants informed him that the enemies had sent men who were entering the town in search of him.

Maruda Pandyiar's blood boiled. He immediately tied the affected spot tightly with a strip torn from his clothing. He summoned his horse and horseman, He had only one weapon, the *valari*. This weapon is made of wood, iron or bronze. Maruda Pandyiar was capable of killing many men with a single throw of the *valari*.

When his enemies surrounded him, it was evening time. Maruda Pandyiar kept killing the encircling men with his *valari*. For some time, the battle went on, with Maruda Pandyiar throwing the *valari* and killing many enemies, the *valari* falling at a distant spot, the horseman fetching it for his leader and him throwing it repeatedly and successfully. He vanquished his enemies, and sped away on his horse, some of the men kept pursuing him, but he galloped away all night without being sighted by them.

He reached a village in the morning. He was tired and hungry as he had fought the pursuers and not eaten anything all night. He came to the *agraharam*, where an old woman was drawing a *kolam* on the ground in front of a thatched house. Some children stood near her. He halted his horse. The old woman looked up. Maruda Pandyiar's royal demeanour filled her heart with warmth.

"Please come, what do you want, *appa*?"

"I am very hungry and thirsty; can you please give me something?" His voice indicated his fatigue.

"I have just *pazhaiyadu*, last night's rice soaked in water. If you don't mind that, I will give you, *appa*." She answered kindly.

"Anything will taste like ambrosia at this point. I need one more favour. I have travelled all night without stopping and I need some rest. So, after I eat, may I tie the horse and rest here for some time?"

"This is not a big thing at all. There is a thatched out-house at the rear. You can tie the horse on one side and lie down there. No one will disturb you, even if you sleep all day. I will give the horse some hay." She served the simple fare of the previous night's rice and vegetables to the king. It satisfied him as a rich feast might have. He spread the mat on the floor and, with the saddle as his pillow, went to sleep. Maruda Pandyiar slept peacefully for a long time. The horse also ate and took rest on the other side.

When he woke, it was noon and the sun was high in the sky. He felt invigorated, and recharged with energy after the rest and food. His heart overflowed with gratitude. He felt that nothing could adequately compensate the old lady for what she had done.

"*Amma*!" he called, "Do you have any sons? Who are these children?"

"My sons have gone out of town for a function. These are their children."

"Do you have any writing implements and a palm leaf? Please give them to me."

"Where will I go for all that? I don't know where they have kept it."

He called his horseman and asked him to pull out a palm leaf from the thatched roof, and a long thorn from the fence. Then he wrote something on the palm leaf. The old woman looked on in amazement. Maruda Pandyiar endowed the village as *srotriyam* in her name, signed it and gave it to her.

"*Amma*, if you give this to the authorities of the Shivagangai Samsthanam, they may grant you some benefit." He then left with his horse and his man.

The old woman intended to show her sons the palm leaf when they returned and to ask them to produce it before the authorities. But she was disheartened when she heard that the Samsthanam was captured by enemies. Maruda Pandyiar was then captured and thrown into prison by his enemies. The chief officials asked him if he had any last wish.

"Whichever village I have gifted as *srotriyam*, whatever gift I have given, must be handed over to the respective persons. This is my only request, nothing else. They also assured him that his request which was an expression of his gratitude, would be fulfilled.

When it was announced that Maruda Pandyiar's beneficiaries would be given their dues, the old woman sent the palm leaf. She received the village as her *srotriyam*. (U.Ve. Sa records that the village is referred as Pazhan Chotrugurunathan Endal) She realized that the person who ate the food she served in her house was Maruda Pandyiar himself. She was filled with wonder that the palm leaf held so much worth. Her heart melted when she saw how Maruda Pandyiar had expressed his gratitude. She was grief-stricken when she heard of his end.

It is not surprising that until she died, she recalled again and again the smiling face of Maruda Pandyiar as he wrote with his bandaged hand on the palm leaf taken from the thatched roof, with the thorn drawn from the fence.

(This story was narrated to me by the Sanskrit scholar of Ramanathapuram Samsthanam, *Sri Saminatha Sastrigal a resident of Tirukoshtiyur, and Sri Muthu Ramalinga Thevar, Zamindar of Aranmanai Siruvayal who lived in the palace of Maruda Pandyiar himself).*

Sankarabharanam Narasaiyar[1]

The Thanjavur Maratha kings were among the best patrons of music and arts, and Carnatic music flourished during their reign, with an increasing number of *vidwan*s who offered a veritable banquet of music. With their patronage, Thanjavur became the royal seat of music.

The Maratha kings won the hearts of the *vidwan*s by their deep appreciation of music, as well as their awards and generous endowments. The titles and the honorifics revealed the expertise of the musicians like Veenai Perumalaiyar, Pallavi Gopalaiyar, Irattai Pallavi or Sanjeevi Shivaramaiyar, Sallagal Krishnayyar, Ganam Krishnaiyar, Tsoukam Srinivasaiyangar and Todi Seetaramaiyar. To these kings also goes the credit of patronising Pachaimiriyan Adiappaiyar, who was not only a great musician himself, but had taught many of the musicians including some of the above.

During Serfoji's reign—a connoisseur of the arts himself—there was a musician called Narasaiyar, who was

1 From the collection, *Kandadhum Kettadhum, Pudhiyadhum Pazhaiyadhum*, 9th edition 2014. U.Ve. Sa Library publication.

in no way inferior to the royal musicians. Once in the king's presence, he sang the raga Sankarabharanam elaborately, with an expansive *alaap* and imaginative Kalpanaswarams. The king and the audience were enthralled, and melted in the beauty of his music.

"We have never heard Sankarabharanam being sung like this!" The opinion was unanimous.

The king gave him many gifts and bestowed the title "Sankarabharanam" Narasaiyar. Thereafter, that was how he was addressed, and this raga was a popular choice at his concerts.

Once Narasaiyar was deeply in debt, and was reduced to borrowing. His efforts to find a lender were in vain. So, he approached Ramabadra Moopanar of Kapisthalam, a generous and wealthy music connoisseur. After enjoying Moopanar's warm hospitality for a few days, he gently broached the subject of his visit.

"I have incurred some expenditure unexpectedly. I feel greatly inhibited about asking anyone for money. And then I remembered you. I thought I could borrow from you and settle that account."

"Loan? How much do you need?"

"Yes. Eighty sovereigns."

"You say you want it as a loan. Will you pledge anything as security?"

"Yes, I will." Narasaiyar said after some thought.

"What will you give as security?"

"One ornament, an *abharanam*."

"Let me see it."

"You cannot see it, you can hear it, it is imperishable, it is a spring of joy, it is my raga Sankarabharanam. I pledge it. Until I return this gold, I promise I will not sing it anywhere."

Moopanar agreed and gave the gold after Narasaiyar signed a deed acknowledging the debt. He returned with the gold and happily settled his debts. After that, he sang other ragas at his concerts, but not Sankarabharanam.

At that time, there lived a wealthy man in Kumbakonam called Appu Rayar. He was a high-ranking employee of the East India Company. Since he wielded influence in Thanjavur and Tiruchirappalli, he was called Ubhaya Samasthana Diwan. Wallis, a British officer, had great regard for Appu Rayar, so he was even called Wallis Appu Rayar. He owned properties in Reddirayar Agraharam in Kumbakonam.

There was a wedding in his family and he wanted to celebrate it grandly, with music concerts by the best musicians, including Sankarabharanam Narasaiyar.

During his concert, Appu Rayar and the audience requested Narasaiyar to sing Sankarabharanam, for which he was renowned. He prayed to be excused, and explained that he had pledged the raga, which unless redeemed, could not be sung. Appu Rayar was astonished to hear this and offered to redeem it.

The *vidwan* narrated the whole story. Immediately, Appu Rayar sent a person with the gold (together with the interest accrued) to Moopanar, asking him to redeem the pledge and retrieve the document duly discharged. The concert proceeded.

That messenger gave the gold to Moopanar and told him what had happened. Moopanar immediately went to Kumbakonam and met Narasaiyar and Appu Rayar. Rayar asked Moopanar if he had received the money and could he have the deed discharged?

"You and the great *vidwan* should forget my act. He has the right to ask me for any amount. Is not my wealth only to help people like him? It was there for his asking. It hurt me that he asked for a loan. So, in jest I asked for security. He offered the raga. It shows his integrity and character that he has not sung it since then. This money is not mine; it is his. You yourself give it to him. Moreover, for imprisoning Sankarabharanam all these days, let this be a penalty for me. This too may be given by your gracious self. Here is the release deed."

"We have seen borrowers returning the loan with interest. But for a lender to return the money along with the penalty is unheard of". Everyone was wonder-struck by Moopanar's large-heartedness.

The next day at the wedding, Narasaiyar sang the redeemed Sankarabharanam. It poured like nectar from heaven on the mesmerized audience.

Thereafter, Narasaiyar became Appurayar's favourite *vidwan*.

What Do You Want?[1]

Of all the Shiva shrines in Tamil Nadu, Tiruvarur is celebrated as the Hridayakamalam, the heart of Bhoomadevi. It is the same place where Shiva is enshrined in an anthill. There we find Sri Thyagesa who was brought by King Muchukunda Chakravarthi from Devaloka and installed. It is to him that more honours are offered than to the other deities. Daily pujas and festivals are conducted elaborately. The evening worship called *tiruvandikappu* at his sanctum or *sannidhi* has a long historical tradition which devotees wait eagerly to watch. Because of this, Thyagaraja is also called *tiruvandikappu* Azhagar.

King Serfoji of Tanjore frequently visited Tiruvarur where he had a palace. He was especially devoted to Sri Thyagaraja. Whenever he went there, he would melt in the beauty of witnessing the *tiruvandikappu.* On one such occasion, the puja was being performed elaborately and at

1 From the collection, *Kandadhum Kettadhum, Pudhiyadhum Pazhaiyadhum*, 9th edition 2014. U.Ve. Sa Library publication.

the time of *Deeparadhanai,* the *arati* and other honours were to the accompaniment of musical instruments.

One such performer was a percussionist called Chinna Thambi. He wore the *vibhuti* and *rudraksham* always; played the instrument called *suddhamathalam* at the Sri Thyagaraja *sannidhi*, and was a great Shiva devotee.

Raja Serfoji watched carefully as each honour was accorded to the deity. When the musicians saw that the king was watching them intently, they played the instruments better than ever. Chinna Thambi also played his instrument. Since he was an ardent devotee, he played the music with his eyes closed, seeming to make no extra effort because of the king's presence unlike the others. His face reflected his inner devotion. The king saw that he was playing the instrument oblivious to everyone but the Lord. He was captivated by the rhythm of the instrument, and the rhythm of adoration in the player's heart. He could see that Chinna Thambi radiated how he had become one with his music, and the king was happy.

"Who indeed will not be overwhelmed by honouring for this deity through a performance? And I am captivated by the purity of this person's devotion." With these thoughts, the king approached the musician. All the others, stepped back respectfully. But Chinna Thambi kept playing with his eyes closed. Raja Serfoji stood there entranced by his music and his appearance. Every moment was sheer bliss.

Finally, he opened his eyes to offer his prayers to Sri Thyagaraja and was startled to see the king next to him. He trembled with fear.

"Don't be afraid! What do you want?"

The percussionist was uncontrollably moved. Everyone including his fellow musicians stood staring at him and the king. Some wished that they had been blessed with this good fortune. Chinna Thambi was struck dumb. The king realized that he was afraid to speak his mind.

"Please speak your mind. I will give you whatever you want, don't be afraid."

The rest listened keenly to what he was going to say.

"Your Highness, our protector, you must grant me a boon. I must be allowed to render the service of playing every day at the *tiruvandikappu* at the Thyagaraja *sannidhi*. This is my only wish. This is enough. Please bless me with this." His hands were folded in respect, and his eyes streaming as he made this request.

The percussionist was well aware that the king was trained in music and that there were many musicians in his royal patronage. So, he was afraid that he would be denied the bliss of performing before the deity, if the king took him to Tanjore. He thought that the king being pleased with him might result in separation from his deity.

The listeners were filled with wonder on hearing his words. The king too saw the strength of his devotion.

"You may perform this service as you wish. Be happy. No one else but the munificent lord, Sri Thyagaraja, deserves your service. You are indeed fortunate." The king directed the officers of the Devasthanam to take good care of the musician. Further, he invited him to the palace and gave him rich gifts, assuring him that there would be no hindrance to his performance of the service.

The people who heard of this incident compared it to the words in *Periya Puranam,* which speaks of Tiruvarur Tirukkootta Sirappu, where we learn of "The valour which makes one reject even moksha when compared to the joy of offering devotion to God out of love.

The Women of Tamil Nadu[1]

The culture and greatness of a country can be judged by the citizens' wisdom, action and wealth. That is why, we have goddesses for these three and worship them.

Just as men are essential for the greatness of a country, so too are women. The proof for this is that the three qualities mentioned above reside in three goddesses: Saraswati, Parvati and Lakshmi in our tradition. If we look at the role of women in these three areas, we can understand their greatness.

Wisdom

Women poets of Sangam times

Wisdom belongs to both men and women. From what we have now, in anthologies like *Purananuru*, composed 1,800 years ago we learn that in the last Sangam age, there were many erudite women. We have the verses of fifty such women and these are as excellent as the verses written by the other poets.

1 Mylapore Ladies Sangam event, speech delivered on 28 January 1937.

Women Grammarians

Grammatical works are more difficult to understand than literary ones. One needs a breath of knowledge to write such grammar texts. The greatness of the grammarians was celebrated by other poets. Kakkaipadiniyar, and Ciru Kakkaipadiniyar are poetesses who also authored grammar texts pertaining to the composition of verses. *Yapparunkala Vridhi Urai* and *Yapparun Kala Karikai Urai* have several references to the works of these two poetesses, but sadly we have lost the complete texts.

Allur Nan Mullaiar

Among the poetesses of the Sangam times, Allur Nanmullaiar was one. She was born in Allur. The Mullai or Jasmine has been identified with chastity. She must have been named for this quality, just like Mallika, and Madhavi are common in Sanskrit. Looking at the metaphors and similes in her poems, she must have been a keen observer of nature, especially of flowers, birds and animals, and deeply appreciative of their beauty.

She compares a parrot holding a neem fruit in its beak to a goldsmith holding a golden coin in his long nails to string on a golden wire. There must have been a round shaped coin in those days. She compares a sickle to the back of a chameleon. She compares a person who does us good, but is later the cause of our sorrow, to the Nerunji flower which is pleasing to the eye, but has a piercing thorn.

Okkur Masathiar

Masathiar was from a village called Okkur. She sings of a *senathipathi* or commander praising a charioteer. The commander loved his wife, but also had to fight a war for his king. After winning the war, he jumped into his chariot and bid his charioteer to take him back home swiftly. When he arrives home, he tells the charioteer," I jumped with joy that the war was over. I only remember getting on to the chariot, I did not realize we had reached home. I nearly fainted with surprise when you said please get down. Your skill is amazing. Did you tie the wind to the chariot or did you convert your mind into that of the horses?" Even in his time of delight at returning to his wife, he was grateful to the charioteer who brought him there. We often say speed of wind and mind. How beautifully this poetess has captured that! (*Agananuru*, 384)

There is a beautiful verse written by her about a brave woman (*Purananuru*, 279).

> What valour! What boldness! She is truly a woman of the warrior community! In that war, the other day, her elder brother died after killing the enemy's elephant. In yesterday's battle, her husband reclaimed the cattle captured by the foes, but lost his life. Today as soon as she heard the war drum, she sprang with such energy! She has only one child, too young to even dress himself. She gives him a spear, clads him in white clothes, combs his hair after applying oil and sends him to battle.

This is the meaning of the verse.

Avvaiyar

We read a great deal about Avvaiyar whose fame is immeasurable. Many poetesses had her name as their name or title in later years and achieved fame. The Avvaiyar of the Sangam age, is the equal of Kapilar and Paranar. Her mental strength is amazing. Her patron, King Adhiyaman once sent her as a messenger to King Thondaiman. The latter wanted to display his military prowess and showed Avvaiyar his palace and armoury. He asked her what she thought of it. She realized that he had no experience in warfare. But without insulting him, she commented on how well-oiled and decorated the weapons were and compared them to the old, broken, blood-soaked weapons lying with the ironsmith of her patron, King Adhiyaman. How brave she must have been, to make fun of that king with such boldness!

Once she visited a philanthropist named Nanjil Valluvar, who regularly gifted elephants to poets. She composed a humorous poem about this, in the voice of a poet who had received an elephant from the king, the summary of which is, "This Nanjil Valluvan knows nothing. There is no rice in my home. I told him that I need some rice to sprinkle over the few spinach leaves plucked from my backyard. However, he gifted me an elephant as huge as a mountain instead. Have you heard of such a thoughtless act? He gave a gift which he thought will enhance his fame."

We have nearly sixty such poems by this great person.

Kakaipadiniyar Nachellaiyar

This was a poetess who composed a verse on how the crow caws as a good omen when guests are about to visit a house. That is why she was given the title Kakaipadiniyar. She composed ten verses on Adukotpadu Cheralathan and was rewarded with gold and other precious gifts. This is in the sixth chapter of *Pathittrupathu*, the anthology of the Sangam period.

Poets from Different Backgrounds

Kuramagal Kuriyeyini and Kuramagal Ilaveyini were gypsy women. Venni Kuyathayar was a woman from the potter community. Their songs are also a part of Sangam literature. It shows that cutting across caste divisions, women were educated and trained in poetics and were scholars. The poet from the community of potters known even today as Koilvenni near Thanjavur. It has an important Shiva temple and was the site of a major battle fought by the Chola king Karikalan. Venni's poem is on his victory and she was well rewarded for it.

Honoured Poetesses

Placing an ornamental crown on the head was an ancient custom of honouring a poet. Ponmudiyar received that honour and has composed a verse on the duties of a warrior. Muranjiyur Mudinagarayar was another who had received this honour. In later times, Sekkizhar and Villiputhurar (who composed the *Baratham*[2]) received such an honour. Ponmudiyar's name in itself is evidence that she received this honour.

2 The Mahabharata composed by Villiputhurar in Tamil.

It was customary for the king to bestow this honour on a poetess or poet, accompanied by the queen. This can be seen from the *Perun Kathai* text and some inscriptions. This shows the ancient tradition that just like men, women were also honoured by the adornment of a "crown" for their poetic prowess.

Young Poets

The names of some of the ancient poetesses end with the term "pasalaiyar"; for example, Kamakanni Pasalaiyar, and Pondhai Pasalaiyar, Marokaththu Nappasalaiar. Pasalai means young. So, there is room to presume that they must have achieved fame and scholarship at a very young age.

The two daughters of King Pari sang a song on their father's death, which is found in Purananuru. All unaware of their tragic plight, these girls were counting the number of salt carts on the road, says Poet Kapilar, thereby demonstrating that though these girls were young, they could compose poetry.

Royal Women

Karikala Chola's daughter, Aadhimandhiyar, has sung some verses. Perungo Pendu, wife of King Bhootha Pandi, who joined her husband in the funeral pyre, composed a verse at that time that is in the Purananuru. The poem proves her values and poetic prowess. It is evident that women from royal families also possessed poetic skill.

Women Poets from Later Times

After the Sangam era, there were many poetesses. One was called Avvaiyar and she composed many poems on good conduct. Her works like *Athichoodi* for children enthuse the young even today. *Athichoodi* is short, alphabetical and easy to learn. Her other work, *Kondraiventhan*, is also famous.

The verses of Andal find a place in the *Divya Prabandham* text. She not only gave Sri Ranganatha a floral garland, but also a poetic garland (a *paamalai*). It is said, that Lord Ranganatha himself accepted her flower garland. Her unfading garland of verses is available for us to savour and learn from even today.

The verses of Karaikal Ammaiyar find a place in the eleventh *Tirumurai*, sacred texts of the Shaivas. They are next to the verses of Lord Somasundara. The saint, Tirugnana, Sambandar has also praised her. Therefore, we can see that her verses are much revered by the Shaivas.

In a village called Karivalam Vantha Nallur, the wife of a Pandya king named Varaguna Pandya, was a scholar and an ardent devotee of Lord Shiva. Here is a verse of hers:

> Our bodies which will rot, is the home of my lord by His will
>
> He is endless, and fathomless and kindness personified
>
> He is beyond all comprehension, and fills all spaces so that even a hair tip cannot penetrate a space that is not His.

He is wholesome and when we think, He is the wisdom within us

He removes our worries and does us good and never fails His devotees

He is like the green tender leaves of the karpakam tree that grants wishes even as we think of them

Our speech and mind cannot define Him for He is radiant and beyond all worlds

But we can easily capture Him in a tiny spot in our minds, should we make a space for Him.

In some accounts, it is said that a Chola king and queen jointly composed verses in Tamil. History records that both were equally scholarly.

The wife of a zamindar of Utrumalai by the name of Pusaithayaar moved to Tenkasi with her two children after her husband was killed in battle, and she lost her land. One day, the older son hit the younger one who complained to his mother. She sang this verse to him—

"To whom shall we complain in this universe?

About our plight—that we who rode in chariots are now on the street.

If we live righteously my dear son, evil will not befall us

Oh! Seevalaraya Marudappa!"

Ammaichi was a lady who lived at the end of the road leading to the Kanchi Varadaraja Perumal temple. She was a poetess. To facilitate the free movement of the temple chariot, her home was demolished. She, in sadness, sang two songs, one is:

"Oh Perumal, you got the snake and monkey to help you destroy the fort of Lanka, did you think my humble home was a fort too for you to destroy?"

Is not her poetic skill evident where she chastises the people who demolished her home as snakes and monkeys?

Kandhiar was a Jain *sanyasini*. She has authored several verses that have been inserted into the *Civaka Cintamani* and other works. What she did was wrong, but reading the poems, one appreciates their high standard. In eight of the copies of the epic, it will be noted as "*kandhiar padal*". Even commentators like Nachinarkiniyar have mentioned this.

One of Kamban's nurses, Utranallurnangai, Thamizhariyum Perumal of Uraiyur are others who possessed great poetic skill.

Women Debaters

There are historical records of wise, well-read women who were also able to debate with others. Kundalakesi was a woman scholar well-versed in Buddhism. One of the five Tamil epics is also named *Kundalakesi*. She was known to have travelled to different places, engaging local scholars from other faiths to debates.

Women in the Epics

Neelakesi in the Jain text *Neelakesi*, Vijayai in *Civaka Cintamani* and Vasavadatta and Mananika in *Perun Kathai* were all highly educated women as recorded by the respective composers. So, it can be gathered that even in those days it was thought that women must be just as highly educated as men.

While describing Ayodhya, Kamban says, the women had large eyes, with a forehead like the moon and they were wealthy and educated so they shared their wealth with anyone who asked and gave grand feasts every day for those who needed it the most.

In saying that beauty, learning and wealth resided in women, the poet also implies that only if the women had these qualities could a country be great.

Musical Expertise

From Sangam literature and old epics, there are several references to the musical expertise of women of those times. Women who lived in the mountainous regions were called Kura *penn* (Kura was the tribe, and *penn* means women). Poems mention how parrots used to faint, hearing the sweet songs the women sang as they watched over their fields. Other references include how they would sweetly sing the Kurinji *pann*[3] as they dried their hair after a bath by the poolside and hearing that, the elephants would forget to graze in the millet fields and freeze in appreciation. We also read that the brave wives of warriors would sing songs to take their husbands' minds off the pain of grievous battle wounds. We read of *viraliar*—women

3 There are five landscapes in Tamil, Kurinji, Mullai, Neithal, Paalai ad Marutham. Kurinji is a mountain. Each landscape has its unique literature, culture, poetry, and more. 'Kurinji *pann*' are songs of the mountain region.

who used to sing and receive gifts from kings, women who used to pray and sing in temples. They used to string the *yazh* and sing in tunes appropriate to the time and verses that brought out their deepest feelings and thoughts and even debate in song.

According to a legend, the wife of Banabhathirar in Madurai, had a contest with a trained woman musician from Sri Lanka and won. It is said that it was a woman from Rajendra Pattinam who set the Tevaram verses in the *pann*s in which they are sung today. Mathangi is the goddess of music. Some women, in addition to their musical expertise could also compose lyrics. A lady named Mayurathamma has composed many meaningful kirtans, praised even by *vidwan*s like Ghanam Krishna Iyer. There are many kirtans like these, by women poets, which are popular in Tamil Nadu.

Expertise in Other Arts

Among the three arts, *iyal*, *isai*, and *natakam* (poetry, music, and theatre), theatre and plays were mostly centred on women. The *Silappatikaram* says that Madhavi was such a great dancer, that several musicians vied with one another to perform for her. Women who served in temples, nurtured this art. In some temples, they had special plays composed and performed by women. In olden days, *Rajaraja Natakam* used to be performed in the Peruvudaiar temple in Thanjavur. Later, the *Sarabendra Bhoopala Kuravanji* was performed, and today during festival times, the *Kuravanji* is performed there.

Among the genres of Tamil texts is the Ula, which is centred around a dancer. They were called *natakaganikai* or *thalipendu*. In the old days, in temples, the following ritual services were performed and sung by women—*ula, kattiyam, echarikkai, unjal, laali,* and *ammanai*. The *Manimekalai* tells us that women were well-versed in all the sixty-four arts.

Medicine, astrology, painting, and sculpture were other arts that women excelled in. Even today, elderly women use herbs to cure family members of diseases.

Women were well-versed in the almanac that tracks astronomical occurrences. They knew many incantations to cure diseases. The kolams they drew are evidence of their mental agility and artistic temperament. They could create beautiful designs out of beads, thread and flowers. They could create boxes out of palm leaves. This practice exists even today in the homes of merchants and Muslims. Women alone are capable of producing artistic work created patiently over long periods of time. With much pride, and persistence, quietly they manage household expenses and accounts—a skill only they can do so well.

The Skill of Women

The ability to bear any sorrow is the biggest evidence of courage. The *Kural* says that to bear with the ignorant is the greatest forbearance.

The greatest strength is to tolerate the mistakes made by the uneducated. They patiently bear the physical and mental harm caused by husbands, relatives, children and others, and even then, keep nothing for themselves and give their all to the betterment of others. The *Perun Kathai,* a Jain epic, says that the greatness of women lies in the patience with which they bear whatever the husband does.

There are many stories of women who have sacrificed all their needs for the wellbeing of their spouse. There are several stories of mothers who paid no attention to their own hardship for the sake of their children's happiness. There are many who have given the best food to their husband and children and make do with what was left.

This verse from the *Natrinai* talks of how, even in poverty, when the woman can live in comfort with her father, she does not even ask for help from him, but instead, chooses to stay with her husband, living on just one meal a day. It uses the word 'madhugai' meaning a strong woman. How strong should one be to live so?

Brave Women

Kannagi is an example of such a brave woman; she is called *Vira patni.* Such courageous *karpu* or chastity is called *veera karpu, marak karpu* and *seeriya karpu.* In her story, we can see the courage of her body and spirit.

Verses in the *Puranaru* record the acts of some courageous women. They took pride in their children who died fighting the enemy. They are called the daughter of Mudhu. The reason why there were brave warriors in Tamil Nadu was because they were fed with heroic stories by their mothers in the days of their childhood.

Physical Training

The physical tasks they did, kept them healthy and were easy on the purse as well. Drawing water from the well, carrying water from the river, washing utensils and clothes, visiting the temple made them fit and gave an aura of prosperity to their homes. Women made savouries like *appalam*, *vadagam* and short eats for their children at home instead of purchasing them from outside, all of which kept them fit and saved money for the home as well.

Games

The games they played suited their nature and growth. While indoors, they could play *ammanai*, *pallankuzhi* to strengthen their nerves and reflexes, playing with a ball was almost an exclusive outdoor game for women. Poets called women as *pandhaar virali* and *pandanai virali*. In some temples, the name of the goddess indicated her love for playing ball games. Kottaiyur is to the west of Kumbakonam. The deity there is Kandhuka Kreedambikai, which is *Pandar virali* in Tamil (*kandhuka* is ball and *kreeda* is game). In *Perun Kathai*, there is a whole chapter called 'Pandhadi Kandathu', where women challenge each other in ball games. So surprising! In it, a lady named Rasanai both caught and kicked the ball. The verse is very interesting. It seems, another lady called Kanchanamala, hit a ball into the sky and then hit that ball with another and similarly made 1,500 such consecutive hits. Then another lady, Ayirapathi, hit the ball with her palm and back hand while simultaneously adorning her hair with flowers and applying a pottu on her forehead, and this she did about 2,000 times. Viswalekai hit the ball with a stick. Finally, Mananikai was the best player of all. The sight of these women is described as they spun round, their hair coming loose, growing tired, their waistlets loosening, the *sandu* dots on their foreheads smudging, and the collyrium too.

Kamban, while describing Ayodhya, says there were designated parks in the city for women to play ball (*Nattu Padalam* 48). He says, while the women played with many balls, their pearl ornaments would fall and scatter on the ground. While describing the women of Mithila, he says they were healthy because their eyes had red lines and their eyes were lined with kohl. Their hands were so red and beautiful that the small white balls on their hands and turned red!

By playing the ball, swinging one's limbs and jumping about, women must have been very fit. While playing ball, they would sing and this was called *kandhukavari.* These poems can be found in *Silappatikaram* and Thathuvarayar's books. Other games they played were: *chazhal, thellenam, thonokkam, kolattam, kummi* and *undhi.* Today, it is rare to see any of these except *kummi* and *kolattam.* Only old Tamil texts mention these. These games helped their physique and their skill in music. They were never idle and therefore suffered no disease. There is a Sanskrit verse that mentions women ate more than men. It was probably because they were physically more active.

Women in Olden Times[1]

The woman heading the home is an old tradition in our country. That is why women are called *ill* and *manai*. The joys and sorrows of a family depend on her attitude. The *Kural* says that the home is made or marred by the good or bad nature of the wife.

A man can give charity only with his wife's consent. This tradition that the right to give charity belongs to the women can be seen in the goddess's shrines at Kanchipuram, Tiruvaiyaru and Senkottai, which show how they nurtured dharma. In the *Purananuru*, verse 163 says, poet Perunchithiranar received a gift from Kumanan and said to his wife, "Here, take what I have brought. Give generously to those you are close to, to those who are affectionate to you, our relatives. Give to those who have given you loans and have not asked you to return it for many days. Give to others you desire to give; you don't need to ask me. Don't think we will live happily by hoarding this with us. Generously give to everyone." To earn was his job,

1 Mylapore Ladies Sangam event, speech delivered on 28 January 1937.

but to give to others and spend was his wife's right must have been his belief.

Hospitality

Women pay much more attention to guests who come home. Both the *Malaipadukadam* and *Cirupanatru Padai* mention how, when guests arrive, and the husband was not at home, women encourage their children to receive the guests by asking them to address the guest as "mama" or "chithappa", which are titles usually used for relatives. Whatever community the guest belonged to, they extended hospitality and served them food. Food, for women, is a vital part of hospitality. *Perumbanatrupadai* has references to how the Panar community were fed and honoured by several communities.

Silappatikaram says that when Kannagi was asked what was most painful about separation from Kovalan, she says it is the fact that she could not extend her hospitality or feed the priests, learned men and the ascetics.

When pining for Ram in the Ashoka *vana*, Sita wonders, "What will he do if he has guests?" This can be seen in *Katchi Padalam,* volume 15 in the Kamba Ramayana.

All these lead us to conclude that the act of feeding a guest was an important dharma for women. Poets speak of a "*virunthu kandu oliththa ooudal*". *Ooudal* is a disagreement between husband and wife. Even when this happens, the wife will not neglect feeding her husband or indeed a guest. In fact, one technique employed by husbands to mend the disagreement was to use that time to bring home guests in the hope that after feeding the guest, the disagreement would also be sorted out and they could live harmoniously again.

Chastity

In the old texts, there are many references to a woman's chastity. Losing their life naturally as soon as their husbands die is considered the highest form of chastity. Self-immolation was the next, and adopting strict widowhood was the last. The Pandya king, Nedunchezhian, dies in grief upon realizing that he has wrongly convicted Kovalan. Seeing this, his wife too dies immediately. This is known as *moothanandam*.

Self-immolation on their husband's death is known in ancient texts as *Ananthapayul* or *Sahagamanam*. In the *Tholkappiyam*, this is praised as the mode adopted by the most chaste women.

Perungo Pendu, the wife of King Bhootha Pandi plunged into the fire when her husband died. When some elders objected, she said, "Why are you discouraging me, when you should encourage me? What is the advantage of your age? What can I say about your scholarship? I am not one who will live after the death of her husband and perform the *kaimai nonbu*. Now, I see no difference between the cool water and the burning fire."

Kaimai nonbu was when women avoided using ghee, flowers, bed and ate only vegetarian food.

Considering Women as Mothers

We do not address all men as fathers. However, with women regardless of age or community, it is our custom to call them mothers. The practice of calling them sisters is a new one. In the old days, except for one's wife, all other women were addressed as "mother". Men would affix their caste names, like Chettiar and Mudaliar. Women would however, be called as *ammai, amma, aachi* and other synonyms for mother. This is the best proof for this sentiment. Karaikal Ammaiyar is an example. Another example is Nachchellaiyar. *Chellai,* her mother's name, is an honorific.

Considering Them Divine

Women, especially chaste women were deified. Kannagi and Avvaiyar had temples for them at one time. Mangayarkarasi, the Pandya queen, is hailed as a divine being by Sekkizhar.

The spot where a chaste woman died would be marked by a stone called the *Masathi Kal.* Even today in our family, occasions like *Sumangali Prarthanai* show how we revere women as divine.

The State of Women in Homes

Women were like workers who kept the home clean and cooked food. Like the proverb, "What will a man who has the plough do? It is the woman's good luck which determines his life." Women were not looked down as mere kitchen keepers, but as persons of good fortune.

Only a woman knows how to live within her means, and she was the finance minister. The *Kural* even says a person who lives beyond their means is an enemy of life. It is the duty of a woman to educate her husband on what the home needs and procure only those items.

A mother is the child's first teacher. She teaches the child its mother tongue. Is there a joy greater than teaching the child the alphabet by identifying things in the home? Possibly, the only greater joy is when we see and hear the child identifying them correctly!

The wife also becomes like a minister to her spouse when she counsels him. There is an old verse which says, the woman has wisdom like a minister. Mangayarkarasi was like a good minister to her husband. Ottakuthar in *Thakkayakabarani* (*Thazhisai* 177) compares both Mangayarkarasi and the minister Kulachirayar to the two eyes of the king.

They are the doctors who care for the health and welfare of their spouses and children. The *Kural* says this as well.

Politics and Women

When they could manage their homes so efficiently, they were really queens of their households. Some were rulers. In the *Tiruvilayadal Puranam*, we read of Meenakshi ruling Madurai as its empress. Rani Mangammal was another ruler of Madurai from more recent times as was Akhilandeswari Nachiyar of Shivaganga.

There were many queens who were highly regarded. In Chola inscriptions, while ending the *meikeerthi* or the lineage and achievements of the king, mention is usually made of his queen who was seated with him. Such queens are called Mahadevi, Perundevi or even Maperun Devi. In older texts, when kings and chieftains were praised, their wives were also praised in the same line.

Principles of Domestic Life

A country was prosperous only because the women had a role in *aram* (dharma and right living), *porul* (wealth) and *inbam* (relationships). Many women attained renown by getting *moksha* too (freedom from rebirth). In the grammatical work, *Tolkappiyam*, the husband and wife are urged to live together for a while and only then renounce family life—also called *vanaprastham.*

Shaiva Women

Many of the Nayanmar saints were able to fulfil their devotion to Shiva only because of the support of their wives. When Sirutondar was even willing to cook his own son to serve a guest, it was his wife who supported him. Ilayankudi Mara Nayanar, Ari Vattaya Nayanar fulfilled their acts only with the support of their wives. Tiruneelakantar became famous only because his wife forbade him from touching her. It was by the effort of Mangayarkarasi that her husband, the Pandya king, recovered and led a good life and the glory of Saint Tirugnanasambandar was revealed.

Sambandar is praised by Sundarar in *Tirutondar Tukai* as a person who was forever at the feet of Shiva and saw no other god. He says that the striped bee drinks the nectar of a half-opened flower or a full, fragrant bloom of the *konrai* flower that Shiva wears, and that is the Shiva whose feet Sambandar reveres and adores. *That* Sambandar has extolled Mangayarkarasi in his verses.

It was because of Tilakavathiyar's devotion to Lord Shiva that the Jain monk Dharma Sena became Tirunavukkarasar. It was Paravai Nachiyar's love that made Shiva go as a messenger on behalf of Sundara Murti Nayanar. Karaikal Ammaiyar and Isaignaniyar, the mother of Sundara Murti Nayanar are revered among the sixty-three Shaiva Nayanmars. Kandrapur is a Shiva temple town, because in the Tevaram hymns, a deeply devoted girl, worshiped the stake to which the cow was tied as a Shiva linga. In the town of Tirupananthal, Shiva leaned over deferring to the wishes of a devotee called Thatakai. Even the temple in the town is named Thatakaieswaram in her honour. Several Shiva temples were built or renovated by the mothers, sisters and daughters of kings. Many are named after them, like Tirailokiyamahadevi Eswaram. Raja Raja I's sister, Kundavai, has made many endowments in Thanjavur and Chidambaram.

Vaishnava Women

Among Vishnu's female devotees, Andal stands out. She is among the twelve Azhwars. Sri Ramanuja was helped by a devotee from the Kongu region called Kongu Piratti. Her descendants live even today. Among the seventy-four *simhasanadhipathi*s, some women are also included.

Buddhist Women

The Buddhist monk, Manimekalai, is remembered by an epic in her name. Women could adopt asceticism, they were called *bhikshunis*. Ancient Tamil Nadu had several *bhikshunis*.

Jain Women

In *Silappatikaram*, we have a Jain monk, Kavundi Adigal. Jain women monks were of three kinds; the ones who renounced before they got married, after they got married or after they were widowed. They would preach to other Jain women. Jain epics end on the note that everyone renounced the world. From this, we can conclude, women also renounced the world. Kandiar was one such woman.

Vedanta *Paatigal* (grandmothers)

Till the last century, in many families, there were very old women who had become well-versed in the Vedantic philosophical texts and would in turn teach them to other, younger women in the family. They were called *vedanta paatigal* (grandmothers). They could very creatively compose new songs with deeper vedantic meaning and teach complex philosophy through melodious songs and simple lyrics. Some of the genres that used to be inherited orally in each family include: *Annai Pinnai, Jeeva Natakam, Vedantakummi, Lali* and *Odam*. These were always orally transmitted.

In this way, women contributed to our philosophy and faith as well.

They Are Like the Pitch of Life

If one collates all the references from Tamil texts, it is very clear that women excelled in all spheres and there are several records as proof of this. Their fame and contribution are just as much as those of their male counterparts. Just as *shruti* is vital for music, women are vital for life. There can be no music without *shruti.* In a music concert, all the applause and enjoyment are for the vocalist and the accompanying musical instruments. One never notices the *shruti.* Women do their duty and serve as the foundation for the success of others and in that way are like the *shruti.*

The Beggar's Song

The Presidency College in Chennai was once a small school called the Provincial School. The teachers of various departments there were all very creative and distinguished. There were famous Tamil pundits like Vidwan Tandavaraya Mudaliar. One of the teachers was a Veera Shaiva Vidwan, Visaka Perumalaiyar. He was an expert in grammar and in Tamil creative works as well. His brother Saravana Perumal Iyer was also well-versed in Tamil. They not only composed many works but republished old rare works. They had several distinguished students. One of them was Tillaiambur Chandrashekhara Kavirayar Pundit.

He had great love for Tamil, and was also well read. His teacher had written *Panchalakshana Vina Vidai and Balabodha Ilakkanam*. Books by others like *Nanul Viruthi Urai, Yapperunkalakarikai Urai, Tandi Alankaram, Vacchanandimalai, Vishaprithi Vishathirattu, and* Arabathar's *Barata Nool* were published by him. He had many students. He worked as a Tamil teacher in Chittor

High School for many years. When Tiruchirapalli C. Thyagaraja Chettiar was on leave for six months, he also taught at Kumbakonam College.

He always had time to talk to other scholars and was never jealous. He loved to learn of the lives of old poets and collect old verses which is something he did wherever he travelled. He would carefully preserve the many letters that contained old rare verses and was always willing to patiently listen to anyone who said they knew some old verses which he would note down carefully. Several of these found a place in his anthology, published more than seventy years ago, called *Thani Padal Thirattu* (Collection of Poems). Today several anthologies of poems are published. The credit for the first goes to Chandrashekhara Kavirayar Pundit.

He was fond of me and I have also contributed several verses to his collection. I used to live in the Tiruvavaduthurai Adheenam in those days where we spent many happy hours when he visited me. By that time my teacher Meenakshi Sundaram Pillai had passed away so, I often cleared my doubts concerning old Tamil texts with him. He was very patient, a thorough researcher and never let the harsh words of others discourage him. He told me many amazing anecdotes about how he collected verses. Let me share one here.

Chandrashekhara Kavirayar Pundit lived in Chennai's Sanjeevarayan Street in Washermanpet for some time. One moonlit night, a beggar who did his nightly rounds for food came along. He was a well-travelled beggar who knew many verses. Instead of begging for food by saying "*amma pichchai*", he would sing Tamil poems in his sonorous voice.

Singing sweetly, he entered Sanjeevarayan Street and many came out just to listen to him. Women, entranced by his music, willingly gave him food. He sang genres like Themmangu, full moon songs, and Paraparakkanni. He would repeat a line several times. In fact, just one such line would do for that entire street. The moonlight seemed to have inspired him to sing a song connected with moonlight.

He began singing: "*Will it burn the town?*"

As soon as he heard the first line of a Tamil verse, Kavirayar's curiosity was piqued; he came out and began to follow the beggar, hoping to hear the next line. The beggar, however, walked the length of the entire street with just this one line sung in different ways. Kavirayar became more and more curious, and impatient too. He waited for the beggar to sing the next line on his own. However, there were no lines but this.

"Why don't you just sing the whole song?" he asked the beggar in exasperation.

The beggar was surprised and noticed that he was being followed by someone of learning and means. He was using that line only to get some alms, but when another—more affluent—person was so interested in the song, he became more wary and a little proud as well.

"Of course, I can," said the beggar and repeated the same line. Kavirayar suspected that this beggar knew no more than one line. After several repeats, like he was revealing a great treasure, the beggar sang,

"Will it burn the world?"

The poet guessed that this was probably a *venba*. He thought, if the first line was so good, how much more beautiful the succeeding lines must be.

"*Ayya*, I have forgotten the rest; it will come on its own and not when I keep thinking about it."

The poet escorted the beggar to his house, fed him and entreated him again, but the beggar was unable to remember the other lines. Try as he might, the beggar could not remember. He did not have the practice of singing beyond the first line.

"Do you know the full song?" asked the poet.

"Indeed, I do. An old man taught me this, but to get alms, one line will do," he said.

"Should you ever recollect the entire song, please tell me, and I will reward you," promised the poet.

The beggar agreed and left. Even after he left, the poet was restless. He felt a strong urge to follow the beggar, just in case he remembered the other lines as he continued to beg. He unobtrusively followed the beggar who kept on singing only the first line. When he reached the end of the next street, the beggar sang the second line of the verse.

"Will it burn the town; will it burn the world?
Whom will it burn? I know not?"

"What a wonderful composition! How beautiful the rest will be, can't the rest of the lines slip from the beggar's mouth tonight?" thought the poet to himself, jumping with joy. Sadly, the beggar had no more to offer that night.

For two or three days after that, the beggar did his rounds again asking for food, while the poet followed him expecting him to yield the whole poem, but in vain. On the fourth night, he had a burst of inspiration and was able to remember the remaining lines. The poet listened to the beggar like he would to a very wise teacher. His joy was greater than that of a man who, after years of prayer, finally becomes a father.

The beggar was rewarded as promised and taught the poet a few more songs as well. The beggar's poem was soon included in the *Thani Padal Thirattu* publication. The full poem goes:

"Will it burn the town? Will it burn the world?
Who will it burn? I know not.
My lady with fulsome breasts like mountains,
Without you, the moon is but a ball of fire to me!"

As the years rolled by, the poet could recall only a few of the poems he had collected. Even so, this one was engraved on his heart.

Rawther[1]

Some Muslims in South India, have the surname Rawther. We find this name in old books and in stone inscriptions. If we study the context in which this word was used, it becomes apparent that it was used to denote warriors who could tame and ride horses. In some contexts, it comes across as an honorific title.

From the *Tiruvilayadal*

Perumpatrupuliyur Nambi was a poet who composed the *Tiruvalavayudaiyar Tiruvilayadal Puranam*. This word occurs three times in that text. In response to Saint Manikkavasagar's pleas, Lord Shiva appears as a horseman to the Pandya king in this text. The incident described in the text is of Shiva giving the reins of the horse to the king. Here the horse merchants are honoured with the title, Rawther.

"Rawtherrayan" means the head of the Rawthers. We can infer from this that Lord Shiva came with several horses and horse traders and that he was their chief. Also note that this word is used by the poet to denote his own God and is indicative of the honour attached to the word. We also learn from the text that the Pandya king honoured the Rawther

1 Published in Darul Islam, issue dated 29 June 1935.

with a return gift of costly garments. Here too, he is referred to as Rawther. There is another story concerning a Chola king. It is about how Lord Shiva appeared as a horseman in answer to a Pandya king's prayers and drowned his adversary, a Chola king, near a waterbody called Kondazhi. Eventually, the horseman, who is Shiva, disappears into a Shiva temple. Here, the warrior on the horse is referred to as Rawther.

Tiru Perundurai Puranam

Tiruvavaduthurai Adheenam patronized a poet called Shastra Saminatha Munivar. He composed the *Tiru Perundurai Puranam*. He, too, mentions the story of Lord Shiva arriving to support Manikkavasagar as a rider. This story happened in Tiru Perundurai, and in the temple is a *mandapa* with an image of Shiva as a horseman, which is called Kudirai Rawther Mantapam.

Kandar Alankaram

Arunagirinathar, in *Kandar Alankaram*, his work on Lord Muruga, hails Muruga as Rawther since he rides his peacock like a horse. In another place, he refers to the peacock as a horse.

Virali Vidu Thoothu

Konappa Nayakan, in his *Virali Vidu Thoothu*, mentions a Rawther as a person who can tame and control a horse.

Kudirai Etram

In the past, the ability to tame and ride a horse was a prized skill and highly respected. Nakula, one of the five Pandavas, and Nala from the Mahabharata were adept at this. Among the sixty-four arts, horsemanship is an essential one. In *Puraporturai*, it is praised as "Kudiraimaram and Kudirai Venri". When the great ancient poet Kapilar met the Chera king, Selva Kadungo Vaazhiyathan, he praised the king as being such a good horseman that he could get a horse to even jump over a moat. Doesn't this show that horsemanship was considered to be a skill worthy of admiration? Agananuru also praises one kind of horseman as *Uruva kudirai mazhavar.*

It was the custom for kings to honour those who were skilled in horsemanship. Later, this became an honorific title for kings and their officers.

Inscriptions

There is an inscription in the Tiruvanaikaval temple (South Indian Inscriptions or SII, Vol. V, p. 428) that reads, "To Rahutha Jajala devar". A certain Jajala Devar seems to have been a Rahuthar, and probably was the king of the tribe called Saupaana as he is hailed as "Saupaana kula tilaka". Rahuthar is another form of the word Rawther. The fact that a king was addressed thus indicates that Rawther was a title for kings as well. Another inscription (SII 169 of 1910) is from Erode/ Coimbatore District. Here, a small chieftain calls himself "Mahamandaleswaran Parvatha Rawther", meaning Rawther of Great Region. Inscriptions show that there was a Tirumalai Rawther who was the Chief of the Palace Guards in Udayagiri and that there was a chieftain by the name of Rawtharayar who was favoured by the Hoysala king, Ramanatha Devar. Amur in Kongu country appears to have been called Rawtherayanallur. Kallakuruchi Taluk also has a town called Rawtherayanallur. It was the practice to name villages and towns after kings and respected persons who held authority. So, we may safely conclude that the aforementioned names refer to such chieftains and personages who were called Rawther and Rawtherayar. From the above literary references and inscriptions, we learn that Rawther is an honorific title that described kings, chieftains and warriors.

Rawt

There is a subsect called "Rawt" in the community called the Balijavaru. They were war heroes of Palayakarar, or small chieftains, and that is why they got this name according to some. Likewise, some of the Kannadigas who were warriors under the Mysore king were also called Rawth. Rawth indicated valour and it is believed to be a synonym of Rawther.

Reason for the Name

The origin of the word Rawther is not clear. Some say it comes from the northern title, Raja Puthra or Royal Son. Others believe *Ra* means horse and the word is derived from that. Whatever the source, there is no doubt that it is a word of honour and prestige. It is a word of honour that denotes a warrior, but how it became associated with one sect of Muslims is not clear. Let me share my explanation. Since ancient times, the kings of Tamil Nadu had warriors from many countries in their armies. Many of the horsemen were foreigners. Even *Perun Kathai* and *Civaka Cintamani* refer to the soldiers speaking a foreign tongue who were capable of handling horses. *Pattinapalai* and other ancient Tamil texts mention horses coming to Tamil Nadu from the north of India by ships. It is well known that the knowledge of horses and trading in horses came from Arabia and that they were experts in looking after horses. When they came with horses to South India, it is likely that many horsemen also travelled. Those warriors were called Rawthers in Tamil Nadu. Since those warriors were Muslims, they and their descendants were all referred to later as Rawther. Even today, in Zamindaris like Udayarpalayam, horses continue to be cared for by Muslims.

In the *Tiruvadavur Puranam*, Shiva appears as a horseman. The author Kadavun Mamuni describes his attire as including shirt, sash and cap, which reminds us of the dress worn by Muslims even today in South India. In the Perundurai Puranam written by the same author, the scene where the Pandya king met the divine horseman is described. The poet says, the king, struck by his beauty, did a "salaam" in true Arabic style! We can surmise that, since the horseman came as a Muslim, the poet described the king greeting the horseman appropriately. This shows the connection between horsemanship and the Muslims of that time.

They turn westwards when they pray. That is where the famed Arabian horses came from. So, it is only appropriate that they have this honorific Rawther, which indicates their skill in horsemanship.

Subramania Bharathiyar[1]

Our habits are influenced by the place of our birth and the people we interact with. Subramania Bharathiyar was born in Ettayapuram, a part of the Pandya region, and a land that belongs to Tamil. In fact, in the olden days, this region was called Tamil Nadu. In Kamba Ramayana, when Sugriva describes the southern country to Hanuman and the others, he says, “If you reach the Pandya country, you will pass the Potigai Hill, and when you do so, don’t forget your task at hand. That hill belongs to Agastya and Tamil is his language. You can easily be trapped in the nuances of his language, Tamil.” Doesn’t this show the greatness of the Pandya country?

While there were many scholars in the Ettayapuram kingdom, when Subramania Bharathiyar was born, everyone knew of the scholarship of the poet, Kadigai Muthu Pulavar. One of his students was the poet Umaru Pulavar. He was a

1 Address delivered in 1936 at the Golden Jubilee celebration of the All India Congress on the occasion when a painting of Subramania Bharathiar was opened in the Chennai Congress building.

Muslim who composed the *Seera Puranam*, an account of the Prophet's life. It is a Tamil epic. In Ettayapuram, many people across the kingdom would recite and enjoy Tamil poems. This contributed to his interest in Tamil from an early age which only ripened as he grew older.

He learnt English as a child. To improve his knowledge of Tamil, he joined the Madurai Tamil Sangam, studied there for a while and began writing poetry when very young. The state of our country had a powerful impact on him. He had a deep devotion to God, the nation and language, and was sad when he met people who did not share this. He did not like those who frittered away their time, lacked initiative and were lazy. He was more and more convinced that he had to say novel things in simple language and set them to music.

He worked as a pundit in the Sethupathi High School and then, when he came to Chennai, G. Subramania Iyer, impressed by him, asked him to work as an assistant editor in the *Swadesamitran* newspaper. Disliking routine jobs, he did not continue for long.

When he was in Chennai, I spent many hours with him. He would always attend the weekly Tamil Sangam meetings at the Presidency College and would recite and even sing his poems. For our annual day, he would compose special songs for us. Once, at a function presided over by V. Krishnaswami Iyer, G.A. Vaidyarama Iyer spoke.

Many were not aware of the former's love for Tamil, or of his scholarship and willingness to promote Tamil, and said, "What does V. Krishnaswami Iyer know of Tamil? Can he speak on such an occasion?"

Krishnaswami Iyer, enthused, said, "What else does one say about this language? It is the language of the Tiruvalluvar's *Kural*, that has been translated into many languages; it is the language of Kamba Ramayana that has all the *navarasa*s; it is the language that the Nayanmars and the Alwars used for their outpourings of devotion."

Among those who were entranced was Bharathiyar. After that, Krishnaswami Iyer asked me to compose and send him songs in Tamil that would increase pride in our country. I did not have time and nominated another person. That person's poems did not please Krishnaswami Iyer, and finally, it was Bharathiyar's songs that he liked the most. It was the speech of Krishnaswami Iyer that inspired Bharathiyar to compose lines like, "the land of the Tamils where Kamban was born."

Bharathiar was filled with the passion that everyone must sing songs that expressed and increased their pride in the nation, and strengthened their patriotism. His choice of lyrics was, therefore, simple and appealing. All of them were soaked in his true patriotism and won him immense fame. In addition to patriotic songs, he has composed songs on other topics and was well-versed in music.

A poet once said, songs are of five types: *Nalikera Pakam, Ikshu Pakam, Kadhali Pakam, Draksha Pakam and Ksheera Pakam.*

Nalikera is a coconut. To eat a coconut, you have to peel the tough husk, break the shell, scrape the flesh and eat it with grated jaggery. Some poems are of this category. Such songs are composed by poets who take their dictionary along with them, and sometimes, despite that, they may be at a loss to explain their own poem!

Ikshu Pakam is like sugarcane. It has to be crushed with great effort to enjoy its sweet juice. *Kadhali Pakam* is like a banana, relatively easy to enjoy—after all, it is easy to peel it. *Draksha Pakam* is a poem like a grape that you can pop into your mouth and chew. The easiest of all is the *Ksheera Pakam* which is like milk. It is easy to enjoy, even for a child. Everyone will enjoy it and it is good for health and for the mind. Most of Bharathi's poems are like milk, like *Draksha Pakam*.

Since he is well-versed in English and Bengali, he has used much of their style and technique. His poems have a high level of self-awareness, much like the old poets of the Sangam period. Grandiose vocabulary and exaggerated metaphors do not always help the poet, and in the past, some poets have been compelled to use them at the behest of their wealthy and powerful patrons.

There are individual poems which extol the beauty of nature, teach ethical values and have lofty ideals. His poems are soaked in his devotion to God and his country.

I want to pay special attention to his prose. They are simple and yet reveal profound insights. They are more important than his songs since they are understood more quickly. They are as easy as his poems. That style is preferred which can be understood without strain. His prose is composed of short sentences, heavy with meaning. We can understand his poems as we read them. *Veera* rasa (heroism) and *shringara* rasa (love) predominate in his songs. He is also a good orator. His songs infuse people with emotions.

His songs are enjoyed by everyone and the proof is their popularity in Tamil Nadu. His songs have spread across the ocean to countries like Sri Lanka, Myanmar and Java. People from those countries have written to me to write about Bharathiar. This reminds me of the praise a poet named Manavai Koothan got for his poem from an erudite listener. The listener said, "Your poem has both a head and legs. Rama's *kavi* (can mean a poet or a monkey in Tamil) crossed only one sea, but your *kavi* (can also mean a poem) has crossed seven seas. Rama's *kavi* had no fetter (*ThaLai*) which is not surprising; however, Manavai Koothan's poems crossed the seas with fetters (*ThaLai*)." Here, *Thalai* means a poetic device. Bharathiyar's poems are an example for the fame achieved, having crossed several seas unfettered.

However much he suffered, Bharathiyar always thought of the welfare of others. He was courageous and his fame is the fame of Tamil Nadu.

Kummayam[1]

While working on the publication of the text of *Manimekalai*, I came across several words that I did not know the meaning of. Over time, as I read other books or spoke to others, I was able to discover their meaning. Sometimes, I had to spend a lot of time and effort to find out the meaning of just one word. Some words I understood through sheer serendipity. Those were joyful moments for me.

In the canto titled *Samaya Kanakkar Tham Thiram Ketta Kaadhai*, lines 175–6 mentioned a word: "kummayam". I was unable to find out its meaning despite asking several people.

At that time, I lived in Kumbakonam. The priest or Patrachariar of the Sri Sarangapani Temple was very well known. He had an imposing appearance and wore *thoda*s on his wrists and always covered himself with a shawl of silk. All important people knew him. He was affectionate towards me and I would meet him whenever I went to the temple.

He once visited my home and asked me to come to the temple. I agreed to do so. Since then, he came home

1 Taken from the Deepavali special issue of *Kalaimagal*, 1937.

several times and would always affectionately invite me. Acceding to his request, I did so, accompanied by Tirumanur Krishna Iyer who supported me in my Tamil research.

We were escorted by Patrachariar, the priest to all the shrines within. Although I had prayed there several times before, I was particularly focused in my prayers that day. Patrachariar explained the history of each shrine. After our darshan was over, he said, "Please wait," and walked to the *madapalli* or temple kitchen. Since that day was an especially auspicious one, several *neivedhyam*s (food offerings) had been cooked for the deity. He asked someone to give small portions of each on a silver platter to us. When I saw the platter, I did not understand the reason for such special treatment that day.

Pattrachariyar gave us the platter with many dishes including *thenkuzhal*, *vadai tirupaniyaram* and *adirasam*. There were some dishes I had not heard of before. As he served them one by one, we savoured it, asked him what it was, and he told us.

He gave me one that I started chewing.

"This taste is new, what is it called?" I asked.

"That is called *kummayam,*" he said.

"What? *kummayam*?!" I exclaimed.

At that minute, I forgot the taste of all the previous food offerings. I even forgot I was in the Sarangapani Temple. In my mind's eye, *Manimekalai* stood before me.

"*Ayya*! *Ayya*! Please ask for more of this!" I requested.

Patrachariar had a larger portion of *kummayam* brought for us from the *madapalli*. It was as if he had already known that out of all the offerings, this was to be my favourite. The joy in hearing and using the word was far more than the joy of eating *kummayam*!

Finding the *kummayam* of *Manimekalai* in the *madapalli*, I said, "*Ayya*! *Ayya*! How much of difficulty I had endured! How do you prepare this?"

For me, finding the meaning of each word is like finding buried treasure.

"How will I repay the great help you have given today?" I asked.

Even he would not have known the value of his help. He thought I meant the food that was given to us.

"What did I do? I just need your friendship!" he replied. We took leave and he accompanied us till the temple entrance.

"There is something I want to tell you" said Patrachariar.

"Please do so," I said.

"The police officer of this town, Ramasami Naidu, is not known to me. I knew his predecessor. I have not had a chance to meet and know him. I am hoping to do it through you. I heard that his son, Venugopala Naidu, is your student in college. Please mention to him about me," he requested.

I promised to do so and took his leave. I also kept my promise.

After I learnt the meaning of *kummayam* from Patrachariar, I encountered that word in the text *Neelakesi* as well. I found more information from other texts and collated them into a footnote in *Manimekalai*. This is what I wrote:

Kummayam—A dish made with soaked green dal and sugar. It is served as an offering even today in Vishnu temples. Periyazhwar's *Tirumozhi* mentions this in 3.3.3 as served with butter. Manavala Mamunigal explains *kummayam* as lentils cooked to a paste consistency. It is also mentioned in *Nanool sutram* 229 as "Payatrathu *kummayam*" and is referred to in the commentary of Mayilainathar.

The European and *Tirukural*

When Thyagaraja Chettiar lived in Uraiyur, many of his students and friends would visit, converse and spend an enjoyable time with him. Authors would request him to write a note on their book. He knew of or would be informed of every special event connected with Tamil.

When I was working towards the publication of *Civaka Cintamani*, I showed him my manuscript. He was very happy to see it and wrote me a letter. I had also requested him to send me any palm leaf copies of this text that he found and he agreed and did so.

One day, a European came to visit him in a vehicle. He enquired the address of Chettiar and stopped beside his house. Seeing this, many in the street gathered around. "Some *durai*[1] has come to see Chettiar," This news spread and others from neighbouring streets gathered as well.

It was at that moment that Chettiar had finished his Shiva puja, eaten and had come to the front *thinnai* with a fan in his hand. He only wore a towel that reached to his ankles.

1 An honorific for an European during colonial times.

A person who was in the vehicle with the European got down and approached Chettiar and asked him, "Are you Thyagaraja Chettiar?" When he saw Chettiar's appearance, it looked like he was delighted.

"Yes, I am. What do you want?" asked Chettiar whose eyesight at that time was failing.

"A *durai* has come in search of you, but you are like this! Can you change your dress and come to receive him? Isn't there a chair here?" asked the visitor with a tinge of authority.

Chettiar had come to take rest, but the person was talking as if some great honour was awaiting Chettiar at his threshold. Chettiar got angry.

"A *durai*? Sure, let him come! Can't he see me like this? Ask him to sit in this *thinnai*," he said calmly.

What could he do? Fearing that the *durai* would get impatient, he escorted him to sit in the *thinnai* of Chettiar's house. Chettiar welcomed him.

"I am not able to recognize you. Did the college principal send you?" asked Chettiar.

"No, I came on my own all the way from Madurai in search of you and I have learnt Tamil," said the European.

The European hesitantly and slowly spoke Tamil. From his speech, Chettiar guessed that he was a priest and replied, "Great! As you read more and more, Tamil language will give you more joy!"

"I have read the *Yappilakanam* and the *Tirukural*. Based on the former, I have corrected the *Tirukural* in some parts and want to show it to you."

Chettiar shuddered when he heard this. "What? Did you correct the *Kural*?" he asked in astonishment.

When he said, "Yes, the rhyming of words did not flow in certain places." Chettiar got angry.

"*Thakkar thakavila renbathavar echaththarkanapadum*" is there—in this, the rhyme is not there. I corrected the second line with "*makkalar kanapadum*". Isn't that more appropriate here?"

Chettiar's hand gesture made him silent. He stood up, shut his ears, hit his head. "How did you think you are better than Tiruvalluvar to correct his *Kural*? What a magnificent work the *Kural* is! Did Tiruvalluvar write it for you to mutilate it? You don't even understand the difference in the meanings of the words. *Echam* and *makkal* mean such different things. Even meeting people like you is not worthy." Chettiar went inside his house and shut the door.

The visitor had not anticipated this. He had, with the help of a Tamil teacher in Madurai, read a few Tamil books. He had read the *Nanool* and was somewhat familiar with the *Yappilakkanam*. He began to check if Tamil poems followed the rules of the latter text. He got hold of the *Tirukural* and found that in certain places, the rhyming was not as per the text. With the intention of setting that right, he corrected them and showed it to a teacher. What could his teacher do? He, after hesitation, said, "You have written it with rhyme, but it is not appropriate to alter old texts without the consent of great scholars." When he asked for the name of such a scholar, the teacher mentioned Thyagaraja Chettiar.

He thought his work will embellish Tamil and everyone will praise him for this. He thus showed his corrections to Chettiar with confidence.

It did not look as if Chettiar would come out again. Those who had accompanied the European peeped through the window and told Chettiar, "He has come all this way to meet you; can you insult him like this?"

"I did not invite him! How will a man who has the audacity to alter the *Kural* be respected in Tamil Nadu? He has insulted Tiruvalluvar himself. His status is irrelevant to me," he said, expressing his anger in words.

With no other option, the European left.

Lives Saved

In ancient Tamil Nadu, there were several territorial divisions. There are many differences between the divisions today and in those days. Tirukovalur and its surrounding areas was a small kingdom called Malayamanadu. It was also known as Maladu.

The hereditary chieftains of that region were called the Malayaman family. They were great warriors and generous with their gifts. Some of the members of this family were commanders in the armies of the Chera, Chola and Pandya kings. Malayaman Tirumudikari was from this family and he was a brave hero. If any king needed help with soldiers, he would approach Kari for support. If any army was supported by Kari that army was sure to win. Therefore, accompanying other kings became his profession. *Thunai* (or the act of accompanying) is also known as *thuppu*. Therefore, Malayaman Tirumudi Kari was also praised as "Thuppin Malayan".

The crowned kings wanted to bestow a great honour on this chieftain who supported their armies and made them victorious. Chieftains were not allowed to have a crown in those times. Knowing that, the three crowned kings decided amongst themselves—"Even if he was a chieftain, he deserves to be crowned. He is the reason why we get to wear our crowns, so it is only appropriate he too wears a crown." Accordingly, they crowned Kari. From then onwards, Kari became "Tirumudi" Kari.

The Malayaman kings were just as famous for their generosity as they were for their bravery. Among them, Tirumudi Kari was amongst the most generous. He gave numerous gifts to wise poets. What gift is equal to that of fighting with the king and emerging victoriously? All the gifts he got, he would give them to the scholars with joy. The strength of his shoulders helped kings to win battles, and poets received gifts.

Enemies feared the descendants of such a brave and generous Malayaman. If they found out that their enemy was supported by the army of Malayaman, they immediately panicked. Due to this, one section of people despised the Malayaman. Among them was a Chola king called Killivalavan.

He lived during the time of Malayaman. He had some young children. Killivalavan decided to destroy the family of kings like Malayaman who were a threat to other kings like him. Killivalavan thought he could live carefree if Malayaman's entire family died. "This is the right time," he thought to himself, "The children in Malayaman's family are now young. When they grow up, they will strike terror in the hearts of the enemy kings. It is better to destroy a thorn bush when it is still small. If I capture them and kill them, Malayaman's family will be completely destroyed." The jealous man went ahead and captured the children

Malayaman's children were captured. Neither their looks, nor their tender age had any impact on Killivalavan. He was as fearful of them as a man would be when he sees young serpents. Who will marvel at the beauty and age if only their venom is foremost in the mind? Killivalavan felt the same way when he saw the children. He ordered that the children be trampled to death by an elephant.

Somehow, the news of the order reached the ears of the poets who had received generously from Malayaman for praising their bravery and generosity. They did not want this fate for the children who were the Malayaman clan's lamps of brightness. Killivalavan saw them as thorn bushes; the poets saw them as young saplings of the wish fulfilling Karpaga tree.

"Is this Chola blind? These children are from the family of brave hearts! How has he agreed to this! What can we do?" They shivered in despair. "Who can tell him?" They pondered for a long time and they were reminded of a poet called Kovur Kizhar.

"If he tries, the lives of the children can be saved!" They decided and approached him.

Kovur Kizhar took up the onerous task. He was respected all across the Tamil country. The soft words he spoke could strike fear even in kings with strong armies.

Arrangements were made for Malayaman's children to be trampled by an elephant. Killivalavan was there with others, watching. The whole town saw the harsh sight and shed tears. Killivalavan was adamant in carrying out his hard-hearted decision.

"Malayaman's family will die today! The family that has been praised by poets always will end soon! Even if these children die, the fame of Malayaman will not! Likewise, the blame on Killivalavan will also not die! Both will be eternal! God has gone blind!" lamented the wise.

The children stood there in fear, looking at the strange place and the crowds, and cried.

At that time, there was a flurry amongst the crowd, as they saw a respected man coming. Everyone gave way to him. Kovur Kizhar swiftly came near the king. The poet took in the scene: on one side was the king, on the other side, the weeping children of Malayaman, and on another side, the terrible elephant in rut, like Yama waiting to discharge an arrow, with its trainer.

The children's voice had become faint after crying for so long. They looked towards the direction of the elephant. They were wonder-struck at the sight of the elephant and stopped crying. When we keep a doll in front of a crying child, isn't it natural for the child to stop crying?

Kovur Kizhar saw this. His eyes welled with tears. He noticed how the tears of the children had ceased when they saw the elephant and this underlined their innocence and childhood. He was filled with pity and turned to speak to Killivalavan.

"A request to your highness, I plead that you lend me your ears," he requested humbly.

"Do you want to do it immediately? Can it wait for us to go back to the palace?" said Killivalavan.

"I request you to kindly listen to it right away and before doing what you are about to do," said the poet.

The king did not have the courage to disobey the poet. Such was the prestige of the poets of those times!

"Tell me," said the king.

"You belong to the Chola race that has been famous across generations. You are from the lineage of Sibi whose greatness is remembered even today. He was willing to cut and give a part of his body to save the life of a pigeon that was in no way connected to him. He was willing to endure sorrow to alleviate the sorrow of others. You are from his lineage. Shouldn't you ponder before you perform such an act? Who are they? Are they equal to you? No! They are from a family who rescue from poverty, those whose only wealth is their knowledge. Any misfortune to them spells misfortune to all poets."

Killivalavan wanted to sacrifice the children because of his fears. Kovur Kizhar reminded him of their innocence and family. Not only that, the poet also pointed out that if Killivalavan extinguished a family that patronized poets, he would be cursed by the poets. The king realized that if he killed the children, he would earn the greater wrath of the poets and it was better to be enemies with the children than earn the wrath of poets.

The poet spoke further, "This act does not befit your lineage. These children are not guilty to deserve your punishment. Let this be. Open your eyes and look at these children. They don't know that they are going to be killed. They are so young and innocent. They were crying because of the unfamiliar surroundings. They stopped crying when they saw the elephant. They see the elephant that is going to take their lives as a toy. Such innocence! Such naivety! Poor things! Are these the people you wanted to kill? Look at them!"

Killivalavan saw the children. The words of the poet struck his heart.

"Poor little children," murmured the crowd and he heard that too. He had seen them as thorny bushes before, but now he saw their infancy and innocence. The poet saw from his expression that he was caught in a dilemma.

"I have said what I had wanted to; please consider all aspects and then do as you desire," he said tactfully.

Killivalavan's heart melted. "Stop! Spare those children!" he cried. The poet ran to the children and embraced them. He had tears of joy in his eyes. The children were scared of a stranger embracing them and cried in fear.

So what?

Their lives had been saved from the Lord of Death!

This is written based on the *Purananuru* verse 46.

The Horse Tamer[1]

Poonthurai is a town in Kongu Nadu's Coimbatore district. In this village there was a brave man called Mattaiya Kuppichi. He was born in the Kadai Kulam clan, which is a part of the Kongu Vellala community. He had a strong physique and great mental strength. He had defeated several others in the sport of mud wrestling.

He embarked on a trip to see and learn about other kingdoms. At that time, a large part of the Kongu region was ruled by the Vijayanagara dynasty. Kuppichi decided to visit Vijayanagara. There was an excellent wrestler there. If any sportsman came from elsewhere, he had to defeat this wrestler and only then meet the king. Else he had to be a subordinate to the wrestler. Above the palace's main entrance gate was looped a long chain. One end of it was held by the left toe. Warriors from other lands had to bow down and pass under the chain. He felt that he was so strong that others had to go past the chain that touched his feet. The Vijayanagara king paid no attention to this.

1 Originally published in the Tamil journal, *Kalaimagal*, in 1940.

If expert horsemen came, the wrestler had a test for them too. He had a wild horse that obeyed no one but him. If someone mounted it, it was unlikely that the person would survive. It would violently shake and turn. If the person was still unfazed, it would gallop to the lake and jump into it. It would then go to the deepest part and attempt to drown him by shaking him off there and return alone.

No one dared to wrestle with him or mount his horse. Visiting warriors would quietly accept the superiority of the kingdom's wrestler, receive the king's gifts, praise the wrestler in the presence of the king and leave.

When Kuppichi reached Vijayanagara, he was amazed by the sights. He also heard about the palace wrestler's exploits. He thought to himself, "*Ada*! Should we bow down and pass under a chain that is touching his toe? Isn't it better instead of returning home? I am surprised there are men who lack self-esteem and are prepared to do this rather than twirl the same chain around his feet and hit him with it instead!"

Kuppichi expressed his desire to wrestle with the palace wrestler. A person looked at his physique and said,

"Who are you? It looks like you are speaking without knowing what happens here. The palace wrestler will not spare you. He will crush you. You look good. Just quietly finish what you came here for and return!"

"I came only for this," replied Kuppichi.

"Ok, that is your fate," he said and left.

The wrestler had grown arrogant with pride since he had not had an opponent for long. When he saw Kuppichi, he was amazed. "Is this fellow going to fight me?" he thought disdainfully.

On the appointed day, the wrestling began. The palace wrestler had grown weak since he had not practised for quite some time, had become overconfident, had been overeating rich food and had gained weight. His muscles were not as taut as before. He had frightened others before, just with his demeanour, but could not stand in front of Kuppichi. He fought with his full strength, of both body and mind, but it was in vain and he lost.

Despite his defeat, he did not come to his senses. He told himself, "I have to destroy him in some way."

"Will you mount a horse?" he asked Kuppichi.

"Yes," said the hero of the Kongu country.

"This kingdom has a horse, whom no one has been able to tame except me. If you can tame that horse, I will accept you as a true hero," said the jealous wrestler.

"Aha! Sure, I can do that," agreed Kuppichi.

Kuppichi had already heard the news about the horse. He was aware that in such situations, physical strength alone would not suffice. He decided to evolve a counter strategy to that of the wrestler.

The horse was brought in front of Kuppichi. He had made a saddle for it and he put that on the horse and mounted it. The next second, the horse showed its wild side.

"Now he will not live, this horse will show him the way to Yama *loka* and this fellow hasn't realized that," said the kingdom's wrestler to his friend and assured himself.

The horse jumped, reared, pranced, rolled, galloped and tried all its tricks, but Kuppichi continued to sit on it fearlessly. He let it go its way and slowly and gently showed it his prowess.

When Kuppichi kicked it in its belly, it sounded like the hit of a hammer. The force he exerted when he pulled its reins seemed to almost tear its mouth. As the horse slowly became aware of his strength, it started foaming in the mouth.

Crowds began to gather at this sight of the horse rider. The king and his court witnessed it from a height. The horse galloped round and round like a cart wheel. The hero did not relent.

The horse attempted it's last strategy. It suddenly galloped to the lake and quickly went in. The crowds ran and stopped by the lakeside.

"*Ayyo*! It is a sin to kill this brave man like this!" Some murmured.

"Doesn't this man know that the lake has drowned other brave hearts?" Said another.

The horse got into the water. Kuppichi did not stop it. He did not tightly hold the reins.

"Why is he allowing the horse to go forward instead of holding it back?" feared many.

The horse descended in the water till half its body was submerged. "Ok, the next minute it is going to shake him off!" thought everyone.

When half its body was submerged, Kuppichi tightly held the reins.

What a wonder! The horse did not go further! It turned and came back towards the lakeside. Kuppichi did not let go of his hold. The horse kicked with its rear legs, circled several times and struggled in the water. Its action showed that it was losing its strength. Soon, Kuppichi relaxed his grip on the reins. It quietly ran towards the shore. When it came out of the lake, it began to do Kuppichi's bidding. Kuppichi easily controlled it and brought it in front of the king.

Everyone was stupefied by this amazing incident. "Not only is he physically strong, but he also has divine strength!" they said in appreciation. The wrestler's face fell.

Kuppichi had already known about the wild attitude of the horse and its habit of taking its rider into the lake. He had collected some lime stone and wrapped them inside a cloth like a ball. He had tied it to the stomach of the horse.

When the horse entered the water, the lime stone began to effervesce. The heat hurt the horse's belly. To relieve its pain, the horse decided to get out of the water. It also feared Kuppichi, and therefore, obeyed him. No one was aware of his trick.

The king invited Kuppichi and asked him about his background. He appreciated his heroism and gave him many gifts. At that time, Kuppichi said, "Maharaja, I have a request."

"What is that?" asked the king.

"Please stop the practice of this kingdom's wrestler looping a chain between his toe and the entrance and subjecting all warriors to walk under that."

His request was acceded to and the pride of the kingdom's wrestler was also quelled.

This story is based on verse 56 of the *Kongu Mandala Satakam*.

The Thief and the Tiger[1]

Among the five great Tamil epics, *Civaka Cintamani* is considered the first. It was the first I published and it encouraged me to publish several other old texts. I learnt many things I was unaware of, because of that text. Since it was a new area, everything was not easily understandable in the initial period. Since it was the forerunner to later Tamil texts, it had many ancient Tamil traditions one learnt from. It is a Jain epic and one can learn much about the religion from it. With the help of many Tamil authors and scholars, I researched it slowly and was emboldened to publish it. I understood many things in the text, that I did not understand for a long time, in unexpected circumstances and from unexpected people.

The hero of the epic, Civakan is born in a merchant family and as he grows up, his abilities become known to the world. Civakan's father is murdered and his country seized by Kattiyakaran. Kattiyakaran does not know Civakan is the king's son, but his fame makes Kattiyakaran jealous.

1 Originally published in the Tamil journal, *Kalaimagal*, in 1940.

A *vidyadhara* lady called Gandharvadattai is in a Jain nunnery under the protection of a merchant called Sri Dattan. Sri Dattan becomes acquainted with Kattiyakaran and builds a *mandapa* and announces, "The one who wins Gandharvadattai in a veena competition will marry her." Competitors from several countries gather there. Sri Dattan escorts Gandharvadattai to the *mandapa* and asks her to play the *yazh*. Everyone who hears her playing the *yazh* are amazed. All those proficient in music come one by one to compete with her in singing and playing the *yazh*. None of them is able to match her talent and thus, six days pass.

Hearing this, Civakan is eager to show his talent in music and comes to the *mandapa*. He is able to win Gandharvadattai in playing the *yazh*. She immediately garlands him.

Consumed by the fire of jealousy, Kattiyakaran plots to kill Civakan. He uses harsh words against the kings who have come there, "Only the one who can conquer Civakan is eligible to marry Gandharvadattai," he says. Hearing this, all the kings unite and fight against Civakan, but they are all defeated. Then Civakan takes Gandharvadattai to his home and weds her on an auspicious day.

This story is told in the third part of *Civaka Cintamani* called 'Gandharvadattaiyar Ilambagam', in an elaborate and beautiful way. Any text has to be studied with concentration, ignoring other things in order to grasp the meaning. I have learnt this by experience, and when I study Tamil texts, I forget the passage of time and get immersed in the meaning of the text. When the meaning is clear, I read the passages quickly. The speed will not be the same, if in some places hindrances appear, and for days, the reading will be stopped.

While reading 'Gandharvadattaiyar Ilambagam', I could not proceed beyond a portion that I was not able to understand.

This was the stanza where Civakan won the music test and the crowds were celebrating, and the jealous Kattiyakaran looked at the assembled kings and spoke to them (*Civaka Cintamani* 741).

In the third line, the poet mentions, "*Kallarar puliyai veru kaniya*". This refers to an episode between a thief and a tiger. Nachinarkiniyar does not mention this in his commentary and I did not understand this. What is the reason for a thief and tiger to appear there? My mind, like a chariot, stalled there, unable to proceed with my research.

The commentary did not have the explanation for these words. I wondered if the author, Tirutakka Devar has compared the thieves to the kings and Civakan to the tiger? If Civakan was compared to a tiger, wouldn't it have been more apt to compare the kings to cattle that cannot attack a tiger rather than a thief? What is the logic in naming a thief? Does the author have some other story in his mind? "What a pity Nachinarkiniyar has not explained this!" My heart struggled with my inability to clear my doubts, and my desire to know the meaning. Since I did not understand it despite some days of thinking, I left the story of the thief and the tiger and continued my research of *Civaka Cintamani.* I tried my best to quickly understand such doubts as and when they cropped up. Unless there was no solution, I would not allow my mind to be fatigued and continue to work and focus my thoughts on the task at hand.

With the grace of God, *Civaka Cintamani* was published in 1887. After the publication, I got some other copies of the text. My research in Tamil also increased. In Kumbakonam, I used to live in Bhaktapuri Agraharam. Adjacent to my house lived an old man called Samba. He was a poor man. On some days, he would eat at my home. When he came, he would talk about his experiences and share stories about those who had been good to him and those who had not. One day, he began to speak about a person he disliked and how that person had caused enmity between Samba and another by speaking ill of Samba. "Somehow, he wanted us both to fight. And so, he said, 'Come thief! Punch the tiger!' Will I be fooled by that?" Samba asked me.

As was my wont, I was not paying much attention to him. However, I straightened at this and asked him, "What is that you said? Thief and tiger?"

"Yes, that person only. 'Come thief, punch the tiger' is how he was trying to get his job done!"

Just as I did not understand the verse of Tirutakka Devar's *Cintamani*, I did not understand this old man's speech! Tirutakka Devar had composed his epic and passed on. I could not ask him what this means. However, this old man was in front of me and he has repeated Tirutakka Devar's words. I could find out the meaning from the old man instead of Tirutakka Devar. I began to ask the question with the same enthusiasm I would have had if I was posing this question to Tirutakka Devar, if he was in this old man's form.

"You said, 'Come thief! Punch the tiger.' What does that mean?"

The old man felt disappointed. He thought, I was going to ask him about the person he was talking about. It was not surprising that he was disappointed because I was asking him for the meanings of some words. The anger in his tone reduced a little bit.

"Oh that! That's an old proverb," said he. But for me, it was a new proverb. "A proverb! What does it mean? Please tell me, it will be helpful," I said politely, as if I asked Tirutakka Devar.

"A traveller with a money bag was travelling through a forest. A thief saw him and chased him. A growling tiger came from the opposite direction. The traveller hatched a strategy to escape from the thief and the tiger. He told the thief, 'Look at that tiger, punch it and I will give you this bag of money!' The thief fought with the tiger, but was killed and devoured by the hungry creature. In the meanwhile, the traveller escaped. He had been able to get both his enemies, the thief and the tiger, to fight with each other and save himself. This is what the proverb says." As the old man said this, unable to contain my joy, I exclaimed, "Aha! Aha!"

I marvelled at how appropriate this proverb was for expressing how easily the Kattiyakaran tried to achieve his end by making Civakan and the kings fight amongst themselves. I was immersed in relishing the metaphor of the thief and the tiger. Though the metaphor had a flavour of its own, its value increased a hundred times because I had learnt something that was beyond my comprehension for long.

I elaborately explained the line, "Kallaral Puliyayi veru Kaniyai", that the kings were vanquished by Civakan like the thieves were defeated by the tiger.

I lost myself in the new understanding of this proverb and I temporarily forgot about the old man. As I came back to the present, I told him, "I will never forget what you have done for me today. Whenever you come home, you are free to have a meal," as I saw him off.

In 1907, when the second print of the *Civaka Cintamani* was issued, under the title, 'Verses That Mesmerised Me', I added the note that "Come thief! Punch the tiger" was a proverb.

Schools of Yesteryears

Gurukulams

Today, there are several books in English and other languages about schools and systems of education. As times change, people's lifestyles also change and schools also conform to the contemporary lifestyle. The education system of those days was very different. The structure of schools then, the status of teachers and the behaviour of students were different. Let me share my thoughts on this in this lecture[1].

In the very old days, the teacher's house was the school. It was called *gurukulam,* meaning where the teacher resides. Similarly, *devakulam* was the place where gods were housed. There is an ancient saying that every village had at least one temple (*ooranor devakulam*). There is another that says one must not reside in a town without a temple (*koyilillaa ooril kudiyirukka vendaam*). And that a town without a temple was bereft of prosperity and unfit to live. Likewise, a town without a *gurukulam* was not blessed. The *Trikadugam* expresses a similar sentiment.

1 Lecture delivered at Sir M.Ct. Muthiah Chettiar High School Teacher's Association, Purasawaiwakkam, on 20 July 1936.

Kanakkaayar

Kanakkayar is a word for a teacher. *Kanakku* is the word for a book. Etymologically, a *kanakkayar* is a person who has many books. It does not mean people who have stored several books in a box. It refers to people who have read many books, analyzed and stored them in their minds. Those, who came to learn from them, were amazed at their boundless knowledge. That is why teachers of excellence are compared to mountains, and while explaining the comparison, elders have said that both have immeasurable magnitude and wealth. They had the ability to teach students according to their need. So, our elders believed that a town without a teacher was cursed. Such teachers were compared to flowers that brought joy to all. Students truly revered them like gods. *Vetriverkai* says that the one who taught you learning is divine. Arjuna praises his teacher Drona as a veritable god, because Drona transformed him from an ignoramus to one whose knowledge was respected across the world. It was an ancient practice for children who wrote on manuscripts, to first start writing on it with a praise to their teacher, "*Nanraaga guru vazhga, guruve thunai.*"

The teachers of those times in Tamil Nadu were well-versed in Tamil grammar and literature, and also conversant of Sanskrit, Telugu and other languages. They had also learnt mathematics, astrology, medicine and music. With a vast knowledge of such wide range, their students could benefit from this. In many towns, the teacher was also the doctor and astrologer.

Those teachers dedicated their whole lives for the welfare of the world. Many poets of the Sangam period earned their livelihood as teachers. The father of the celebrated poet Nakkeerar was a *kanakkayar* too. People respected him so much that they did not utter his name. Even today, we know him only as Madurai *kanakkayar.* We also know of another Sangam poet called Kanakkayan Dattan, who was a teacher.

Thinnai Pallikoodam

The village school is called a *thinnai pallikoodam* or *thetri patasalai.* A broad dais was set up under the shade of a large tree in a common place in every village. It was called a *manram* or *ambalam.* People gathered there to discuss matters concerning the village. Since one could stay and be sheltered against the sun and the rain, visiting musicians availed of this space. I would surmise that classes were conducted in the spaces on the platform under the tree shade.

Manram

In the Sangam work *Kuruntogai,* there is a verse about a girl and a young *panan.* A *panan* was an itinerant musician. The girl looks at him and wonders, "He is a young student; what will he be like in his village *manram*?" This tells us that students studied in *manrams*. The *manram* was just the platform or *thinnai* under a tree. It probably then became the *thinnai pallikoodam.*

In ancient times, students learnt close to nature, under trees or in the groves. Now we bring the plants and shrubs where the schools are and create a grove. Just as we paint forests on the screens used for plays, we now rear plants in pots and at the entrance in schools.

Palli

The classes under the trees slowly moved to thatched huts. Many *mathas* became schools. The word "*palli*" was used both for Jain monasteries and schools.

Places of meditation were also commonly called *palli*, because they were places of learning and teaching. They did not differentiate between schools and *mathas* so they were commonly called *mathas*. Old inscriptions reveal that students stayed in *mathas* to study specific books. A stone inscription records that during the reign of Rajaraja Chola II, there were students in an old *matha* of Tiruvavaduthurai who studied the grammar text *Rupavataram*. Lands had been endowed for that purpose. Similarly, there were pathshalas teaching Vedas and Agamas in many *mathas*. Another inscription tells us that in Tirumukkudal in Thondai Nadu, there was a *pallikoodam* where many students studied medicinal texts.

Tamil Pallikoodam

Though not many records speak of Tamil *pallikoodam*, if we analyze the traditional practices we know that they existed in every village. It had been the practice in Tamil Nadu, from ancient times for many students to get together and learn from one teacher. We know that Agastya had twelve students. All the twelve were students of one *salai*. *Salai* means *pallikoodam* and they studied in one school under one teacher. But we cannot say with certainty that there were only twelve students. Hundreds of students may have studied, but of them only twelve gained fame. Did not hundred and five learn from Drona?

Teacher's Qualification

The teachers owed the responsibility to teach their students life lessons and not just bookish knowledge. They also ensured formation of their students' character, so that they do not transgress ethical codes. Teachers, by their own conduct, were role models. Not everyone can be a teacher. Only those, who by the merit of their previous births possess great learning, good conduct and divine grace, can be teachers. They were great reformers and even kings were afraid to earn their displeasure.

It is true that wealth earns respect. But ordinary wealth pales into insignificance before teachers who bestow on this world the wealth of education. There is nothing that will not be submissive before a teacher; even wealth and valour bow before a teacher.

Civakan

Tirutakka Devar speaks of how Civakan acquired learning. Nachinarkiniyar, in his commentary, writes that he learnt without the arrogance of his wealth. Wealth bows down to learning.

When Civakan realized his true state, he was filled with a fervour to conquer his enemies immediately. When his teacher asks him to wait for a year, immediately he calms down and does his teacher's bidding.

Arjuna

The great warrior Arjuna stands at the forefront of the army in Virata Nagara to retrieve the stolen cattle. Drona comes before him. When Arjuna sees him standing with his foes, his hands let go of the bow and arrow and join together in respect to his teacher.

"Oh, king of Brahmins! By your grace, we are well and have completed our exile in the forest. Your teaching has made me a great archer; you are divinity in human form for me. To fight against you is a crime," he says respectfully. His bravery shrinks before the teacher.

"No, my child. I heard that you defeated and killed the *nivathakavachakalakeya*s. I desire to see your valour in action. I stand on this side, because I am beholden to them. May you fight fearlessly!" Arjuna picks up his weapons only after he hears these words of his teacher.

If teachers possess such greatness as to command the respect of excellence of all kinds, how superior should their qualifications be!

Oru Salai Students

In a *gurukulam*, the students interacted forgetting the differences in status. The emperor and *bikshu* were the same.

The Mahabharatha narrates the story of Drupada, the prince of a big empire, and Drona, the poor Brahmin, who were classmates and friends studying in the same pathshala. That friendship should have remained unchanged throughout their lives. Drupada did not do so and hence suffered untold misery.

Krishna, a king, and Kuchela, a pauper, were students in the same school. *Kuchelopakyanam*, the story of Kuchela, tells us how the bond of friendship stayed close all their lives.

During the student days of my teacher Meenakshi Sundaram Pillai, a classmate would unfailingly borrow his books, but would forget what he read. Many years later, Pillai had become the *vidwan* of Tiruvavaduthurai Adheenam and was celebrated all over Tamil Nadu as a poet extraordinaire. When, one day, he was walking along the road with his students, I was one among them. That school-friend saw us. He looked very ordinary. When he saw our teacher, he addressed him just by his name. We had never heard our teacher being addressed with such familiarity, and were startled. Both of them conversed with each other with great warmth. After he left, our teacher saw the curious and meaningful glances being exchanged among us, and explained that he was a childhood friend. Though there was a difference between them, like that between a mountain and a molehill, we understood that the years together in school had formed this close a bond between them.

The Training in School

The *gurukulam* students got food as alms, gave it to their teacher and ate what remained. That very practice taught them humility and patience. This inspired great respect in the townspeople. The duty of parents ceases after the children are born. It is the teachers who educate the children to become good human beings and enrich their lives. When Viswamitra wanted to speak about the upbringing of Rama and his three brothers, his words were, "Dasaratha is just called the father of the four, but in truth, it is Vasishta who nurtured them so that the whole world benefited by them." There is no use if the father bequeaths wealth and riches to his child. It is education that helps the child to employ the wealth beneficially. A father's foremost duty is to educate his children. Even a royal prince will shine in later years, only if his skills are honed at a school. A poet has written about a man cursing his father because, though he was born with wealth, he was reduced to depths, as his father had failed to correct him in his youth and send him to school.

Until the last century, we had *thinnai* schools. I had only studied at such a school. The years I spent learning Tamil from Sri Pillai was really a *gurukula vasam*. Many like me gave up everything for the sake of studies and learnt from him. Sri Pillai had close contact with the village school-teachers. The teacher could rein in boys who could not be disciplined by their parents. The boys were entrusted with the teachers as soon as they were capable of learning. From then, till they reached manhood, they forgot the material world and focused only on learning.

Starting to Learn

When the child was five, the parents entrusted the child to the teacher to teach the alphabets. The children started with the words "Om Namasivaya" or "Om Namo Narayanaya". The Jains started with "Om Jinaya Namah". The custom was to start on Vijayadasami, as it was believed that it would bring in the grace of Saraswati, the goddess of education.

The child's first day at school was celebrated as a special event. The teacher was offered many gifts. On a plank, turmeric was spread and puja was offered to it, then the child wrote on it. The teacher would recite the alphabets in order and the student repeated it. This practice of students repeating what the teacher said was called *muraivaippadu*. There was a *sattampillai* or a boy who supervised the students. Sometimes, he did the *muraivaippadu*. After this ceremony of teaching the alphabets, every time a new text was taken up for study and it was celebrated in a small way. This was called *suvadi thuvakkal.*

Maiyaadal

They wrote with a special ink or "*mai*" so that the words were legible on the palm leaves. This was made with sweet flag root (*vasambu*), turmeric, juice of black night shade (*manathakkali*) or thorn apple (*oomathai*), soot from mango leaf, and soot from *darbha* grass. Not only did this *mai* make the words look clear, it was also beneficial to the eyes. Since the study of the alphabets began by reading what is written with *mai,* the event was called *maiyaadal vizha.*

The epic Cintamani says, "*Aiyaindeydhi maiyaadi arindaar kalaigal* (He acquired learning after the age of five and the *maiyaadal* ceremony)."

A poet who personified Tamil as a child in his work *Tamizhvidu Thoodhu* also refers to this custom of spreading turmeric and *maiyaadal,* and says that the child grew beautifully by being bathed in turmeric and adorned with *mai.*

When all the children repeated what the teacher said, different tones and voices could be heard in chorus. Kamban has compared it to the cacophony of frogs. Even *Sethu Puranam* speaks of students reciting the alphabets loudly in order. Near the mountain Gandhamadanam, students were reciting the Tamil letters. When they said "*vaa* (come)", they heard the echo and looked around to see who was calling them. When they said, "*po*", they heard the echo and wondered who was telling them to go. When they shouted "*coo*", they heard the echo and were alarmed to hear the cry. This is the scene from *Gandhamadana Padalam.*

Writing on the Sand

The children first practised by writing on sand. The letters were then formed clearly and in a straight line. The teacher first wrote on the floor, the students repeated it and kept practising to write. This practice of writing on the floor is described in the author's dedication in *Kanda Purana*. "My attempt to write the epic on Lord Muruga is like a young boy attempting to write a book before he has even practised a little to write on the floor." The poet is telling us that the first stage in a student's education is writing the alphabets on the floor, it is only at the mature stage that he can write a book.

There is an old *venba* that says the written letter shall not be crooked or slanting, but straight like an arrow. In the olden days, the letters were written without touching each other and in a straight line. This will be apparent from old manuscripts. Looking at such writing, poet Kachiyappa Munivar, in his poem, *Thanikai Puranam*, has compared the well-aligned letters to a row of mansions on a road in a big city. Each letter has its special form and the letters stand in a line; similarly, each mansion had its special design and the mansions stood in a row. Many letters form a line, many lines form a page, many pages form a book. Similarly, many houses are in a street, many streets form a division and many divisions form a big city.

Formation of Letters

The shape of letters remained unchanged for a long time. The use of dots and other devices to indicate long vowels are features of this. Because of the training given by our elders, the shape of letters have not changed even though several centuries have passed. The formation of letters in the grammar text, *Tolkappiyam*, and the *Nannool*, which came hundreds of years later, reveal very little differences. The author of *Nannool* stresses this aspect. When things change daily in the present times, it is because of the school practice from those times that has resulted in Tamil letters not undergoing drastic changes.

The great scholar, Meenakshi Sundaram Pillai, compares the *kodu, kaal, pulli* and *vilangu* that are the limbs of the Tamil letters *(nedunkanakku)* to the Naimisa forest in his *Mayurapuranam. Kodu* also means branch, as trees have branches; *kaal* is foot—you have the foot of a tree which is the base of a tree; *pulli* is a dot—there are trees that have such marks; and *vilangu* is a curve or a bend—trees have them too.

Memorization

There is a big difference in the method of teaching then and now. The students memorized the basic texts. In Tamil, they knew by heart the *Nikhandu, Nannool, Kaarikai, Thandiyalankaram* and other moral texts. There were several tables in arithmetic, like *kizhvayilakkam, melvayilakkam* and *kuzhimatru,* which had to be memorized. The Sanskrit text *Amaram* had to be learnt by heart. In the olden days, it was considered very important to sharpen the memory skills. And there were many methods to do that. If you note the *ghanam* and *jata* methods of learning Veda, that too indicate the importance of learning by heart. The phrase "*thalaikizh padam*" means learning it back to front.

Teachers adopted some methods to improve the memory power of children. When the children were leaving to go home, the teacher told them the name of a flower, vegetable, fruit, beast or bird, and they had to repeat it the next morning. As soon as the children went home, they repeated the words to their mother, and they too saved it in their mind. When they woke up, early next day, they recalled it. Then they repeated it to their mothers to verify if that was correct.

The children's texts, like *Athichoodi* and *Kondraivendan,* are set in alphabetical order only to facilitate its ease of memorizing. In the same way, the *anthadhi* (first verse ending with the letter that starts the second verse), the *edhukai-monai* (rhyming of the first letters of each line or the last letters) jogged their memory to remember verses. Learning *andhadhi* texts at a young age was only to aid the memory. *Nikhandu* is set to *edhugai* only for this purpose. The texts had *muthal ninaippu,* which was a verse composed with the first word of every verse in the text. So, students memorized this *muthal ninaippu* to aid their memory. *Yapperun Kaarikai* has *muthalninaippu* verses, Sanskrit texts like *Rupavataram* also have them, and they were called *neethaka slokam*. The *adivaravu* in *Divya Prabandham* was a similar tool.

The school children would keep revising in their minds the lessons they have learnt. Many would do joint studies where one asked questions and the other answered. By such means, their learning process continued without any hault.

It was easy for them to speak about a subject without the help of books or notes, to explain the meaning of a verse and to explain with reference to the context. In those days, there was a practice for one student to recite a verse and the next student starting to recite a verse beginning with the same letter with which the previous verse ended. This would continuously go on like a chain of recitation. They constantly recite these verses while walking, plucking flowers for their teacher's puja, while stringing the flowers for garlands or for stitching leaves for eating.

Even when alone, they practised this. If they forgot the lines, they immediately looked at the text to remind themselves. For this purpose, they always kept the texts with them, and in fact, "never to let go of the text" was itself repeated as a saying.

Rising Early in the Morning

Students got up early in the morning to study; this habit was instilled in them by their teacher. Some children came to their school when the first cock crowed. Since the teacher caned latecomers, all the students got up early and in fact they woke up their sleeping parents. When the teacher started the lessons, the students were made to stand according to the order in which they had come to school. The student who came first was called *vethaan* or *ethan*. The teacher would gently touch his hand with the cane. He would stroke the hand of the student who came next. The force of the cane would increase gradually and the boy who came last would be severely beaten. Fearing this punishment, the students came to school very early in the morning. The boy who came last on the previous day would be at the school first on the next day. He would clear his throat as soon as the next person came so that the other should not think he was the first to arrive. In those days, lying was not a habit. The boy who came later would not say that he was the first to arrive.

Manuscripts or Palm Leaves

The boys preserved their palm leaf manuscripts carefully. For the very young students, the teacher snipped and carefully cut the palm leaves and strung it with a thread. Sometimes, one hole was made in the palm leaf, and sometimes, two. The other students did this themselves; they used to write on palm leaves or *seethala* leaf. The manuscripts of those days remained intact for many centuries. On the top leaf of the manuscript, they drew many drawings. As a frame on the top, they fix the stem of the palm leaf or by a strip of wood or copper. These were beautifully illustrated with colours. In the two old manuscripts, they tied one hole with a copper wire or a bamboo stem. This was called *naraasam*. These manuscripts were in different shapes somewhere in the form of cylinders. I have even seen some manuscripts in the shape of a Shivalinga. One end of the string with which the manuscript was strung was cut like a parrot's beak, so that the leaf would not come loose. This was called *kilimookku*.

There was a method for tying the manuscripts. The teacher distributed the leaves among the students to test whether they tied them properly. There were as many different sizes of palm leaf manuscripts as there are in printed books today.

Preservation of Manuscripts

Apart from taking care of the manuscripts and checking them regularly, the people in those days took all the manuscripts that they had studied and arranged them in order on Saraswati Puja. Even those who were engaged in different occupations took up their books in their house at least once a year and cleaned them and protected them. Now we bind our books. Is it not? In the same way, they would replace the string and the strip with new ones. If a manuscript had become very old, they would make a new copy. (This is the reason why there are some differences in the texts of very old manuscripts). Then they would ink it again afresh. This is how the books in those days remained in good condition without damage. After making copies, if the old manuscript had become too damaged, they would dip them in ghee and according to the rules, they would offer them in the homa fire. Otherwise, they would drop them in the river on padhinettam perukku (18th day of the month *Aadi*). This was *parikaram* or the ritualistic disposal of damaged manuscripts. Now we have to condemn all manuscripts by *parikaram*, since we had failed to adhere to the old practice of making new copies before parikaram of the old ones.

Writing Tools / Stylus

There were different kinds of styluses fit for writing on manuscripts. It was also called *oosi*. There were several kinds called *maddaku ezhuthaani, vaar ezhuthaani and gundu ezhuthaani* et. These pens had a knife at one end for sharpening and the other end was for writing. Perhaps, the genesis of the word "pen knife" is from this. There were styluses which had two knives at one end and two nibs in the other.

How to Write

In those days, they had very thin nibs to enable writing twenty–thirty lines on one page with very fine letters. The scribes would hold the pen in their right hand and palm leaves with the left hand. While writing, they would make a little dent with the left thumb nail and write by pressing the nib in that dent. They could write swiftly just as we write on paper today. No one writes on palm leaves in schools nowadays. But here and there, that practice is still in vogue in some temples and some jewellery shops. In the olden days, documents like sale deeds, gift deeds, partitions, mortgages and agreements and other calculations were written only on palm leaves. To make their students acquire good handwriting, the teachers wrote words on the top of each student's manuscript. They had to copy this and it was called *sattam*.

Thookup Palagai

The implement in which manuscripts were kept and carried was called *thooku*. In the play *Thooku Thooki,* the prince carried the manuscript *thooku*s and hence got that name. It was also called *asai*. The writer of *Tamil Viduthoodu* has beautifully compared this *thooku palagai* to the cradle on which the Tamil child is laid.

Respect to the Teacher

Students in those days got up early and walked to the river carrying the twigs with which they would brush their teeth. After brushing their teeth, they carried the river sand while saying their prayers, and attended school after paying respects to the teachers. This practice may seem strange to everyone today. The teacher was considered as one of the *aimperum kuravar* (the five superior preceptors). The student performed whatever was required by the teacher.

Offering to the Teachers

Every day, the students brought to the teacher some offering, depending on what the family could afford; some brought vegetables, some brought milk, and if even that was not possible, they would at least bring one log of firewood. Though the value of their offerings differed, the teacher had the same love towards every student. The biggest fee received by the teacher was something like a quarter of a rupee. Yet they did not think that their life lacked anything. On special days, they received many kinds of gifts. The *Ulaganeethi* verse says, "Do not delay the payment of the teacher's fees." *Tirupughazh* says the person who does not pay his fees to the teacher would suffer in seven hells. From all this we learn that teachers did not have to feel any anxiety about their livelihood and that the people thought that it was their prime duty to take care of the teachers.

Holidays

The holidays were *pournami, amavasai, ashtami, prathamai*, special festivals and special temple festivals of the town. On those days, the students would spend their time happily together. These holidays were called *vavu* or *uvavu*. *Pournami* and *amavasai* were called *uvavu*. Since those two days were holidays the other holidays also got that name. On the nine days of navaratri, there were special events like *kolattam*. At those times, the people would give money to the teachers. Even today, in some village school teachers get special pay during navaratri.

Punishment

Many kinds of punishments were given to students. In later times, since less educated people became teachers, horrible punishments like *kothandam iduthal* (the use of rope to punish them), *annanthaal poottuthal* putting the student in chains, using canes also began. Those teachers took advantage of the phrase, “If you raise the stick, the monkey will dance.” These people who compared the unparalleled work of a teacher to a monkey trainer were different from teachers of olden times.

The Punishment of Carrying Weight

One kind of punishment was to make the student who failed in verse recitation to carry the students who passed. It appears that this existed in olden days. One of the *tiruvilaiyadals* of Lord Somasundara of Madurai is called *isaivaadu vendra tiruvilaiyadal* (the divine event relating to winning the music competition). In this, we come across two women who play the veena competing with each other in a contest. The winner was a Shiva devotee and the loser carried her. This is found in *Tiru Alavayudayar Tiruvilaiyadal Puranam.*

Controlling the Students by Love

In the olden days there were no severe punishments. The teachers disciplined their students in the right way by love and affection. The students had respect for the teachers and were afraid of them. Sometimes, they were so confused that they did not know they had committed errors.

In the *Perun Kadai*, King Udayana played the instrument *yazh* and controlled an elephant in rut. He mounted the elephant and made the elephant pick up the elephant goad and hand it over to him. Just as an elephant in rut submitted to the melody of the *yazh* but not many weapons, students submitted to the affection of the teacher. Elders have compared the manner in which students interact with their teachers to a person who is feeling cold sitting before a fire not too close, but not too far.

Debate

In our schools, the educational system had debates. In Sanskrit, this is called *vakyartha*. Scholars demonstrated their knowledge by debating in the royal court. From the Tamil texts like *Madurai Kanchi,* we learnt that for this purpose, these people held a banner or a flag. The debating practice developed from school days itself. An old *sutra,* after describing the manner in which a student acquires education, concludes with the words that the habit of raising objections and giving explanations matures into debating skills.

A Lifetime of Learning

The people of our country did not stop their learning with their school days. Tiruvalluvar in his *Kural* says that one should continue learning till one dies. It is the basic habit instilled in school that makes one's life rich and beneficial. After school education concluded, the people of olden times sought teachers who would teach them subjects which they had not learnt and acquired knowledge in those subjects. My Tamil teacher Sri Meenakshi Sundaram Pillai educated himself like that. Paranjothi Munivar compares such students who seek education in different disciplines to the gentle wind which carries the fragrance of many flowers.

Separation Known as *Odham*

In those days, even after marriage, people went to other places to teach what they knew, to take part in debates and to learn subjects that they did not know. In *Tolkappiyam* and other ancient grammar texts, this period when the student separate from his partner to study is called *odhar pirivu*. This period of study was for three years. Many learned scholars from places like Nava Dwipam came to Tamil Nadu to pursue their studies. From an inscription in Tanjavur of the period of Raja Raja Chola I, we learn that many students from foreign countries came to Thanjavur to learn from Sarva Shiva Pandithar who was a great scholar in Agama Shastra. It will not be an exaggeration to say that his house was an Agama college of those times. Tiruvavadu thurai *matha*, Dharmapuram *matha* and others functioned for a long time as Tamil colleges. We see that in Tamil Nadu, there were places where people of all ages could learn, from schools for children to schools for elders. What is called Tamil Sangam is really one kind of institution of research, is it not?

Epilogue

These schools have undergone a change over time. When we think of the values generated by them and the wealth of books accumulated by the scholars who studied there, we are filled with pride. We yearn to return to those days. Even if those methods are not revived, let us at least learn the basic values of those schools.

Musical Instruments[1]

Among the three kinds of literature (that which was read, that which was sung and that which was acted), the Tamil people attributed pride of place to music. The written Tamil that is *Iyal* was in the form of verses or *seyyul* and had to be learnt with music. It is well known that music is indispensable for plays. Only those who are learned in Tamil grammar, or know English or Telugu are enthralled by the works of experts of Tamil grammar, English and Telugu. But music enchants all living beings, the lettered, the unlettered, animals and even birds. It is often mentioned in ancient Tamil literature, that even the insentiate creatures were enchanted by music.

During the season when the flowers in the forest bloom, the bees enter and drink the nectar. The bud that is about to bloom is called *podu* (time) in Tamil. By just looking at which *podus* were in bloom, the forest dwellers and the sages could find out the time of the year. There is a flower called *Nallirul nari* (literally fragrance of the night) that

1 Talk given at the YMCA hall, for summer music school, on 16 June 1929.

blooms only in the middle of the night. Though the sun has disappeared, since the flower indicates the time of day or *podu*, by blossoming and closing, those ripening buds were called *podu*. When the bees hum or sing near those *podu*s they would bloom. The *Kurunthokai* says, the flowers gently opened their mouths for the bees.

It is said that snakes are charmed by music. Elephants roaming in rut are also tamed by music. Poets sing of elephants, which cannot be controlled by weapons like *parikkol* and *kuthukol* are calmed by music. Such metaphors can be found in the *Kalithogai, Perunkadhai* and *Merumandara Puranam.*

The *Agananuru* speaks of an episode of a girl in the Kurinji region who is guarding millet fields. After taking her bath in the clear pond, she goes to the raised platform, gently drying her hair, and starts singing the songs native to the Kurinji region. An elephant comes there to feed on the crops, but is so enchanted by the music that it forgets its ravenous hunger and entranced by her music, stands still. In *Perungakadhai,* we find that Udayanan controls the enraged elephant called Nalagiri by playing the veena, and then mounts on to it with his weapons and rides it. Describing the manner in which the elephant is subdued, the author says that the elephant was as submissive to Udayanan as a student is before the teacher.

The story of Krishna tells us that cows were enchanted by music. After having let the cattle graze wherever they please, Krishna does not do anything when he has to drive them back to the village; he just has to play the flute. At once, all the cows gathered towards Krishna from wherever they were. A divine poet has briefly described this scene. The *Periyapuranam* also relates such scenes while telling the life story of Anaayanaayanar.

Asunama is an animal, some call it a bird too. It could understand and listen to music. It rejoiced in sweet music and would faint on hearing music that was not melodious. References to this can be found in the *Agananuru, Civaka Cintamani* and Kamba Ramayanam. We learn that those who wanted to capture it hid themselves and played the *yazh*; the *Asunama* on hearing the music would come out to listen and get caught. The hands that played the *yazh* and enchanted the birds, were the same hands that endangered their lives. This simile is used by a Natrinai poet. The *kinnara* bird is also like this.

Even today, we see the cattle being used to pull the carts and to draw water from the well, doing their work calmly and smoothly, listening to the *temmangu* and *etram* songs. That *temmangu* is like a stream of honey. Who does not know the magic of the mother's lullaby soothing the crying child, lulling her to sleep?

Even hard-hearted robbers lose their hearts to music. Such a story is narrated in an old book. In the *Palai* regions the highway robbers waylaid the travellers and took their lives and wealth. Even if the travellers had no money, they killed them for the sadistic pleasure of cutting and seeing the torsos writhe. However, when they heard the bards' desert songs, the robbers let the weapons slip from their hands, forgetting their cruel deeds and enjoyed the music.

Civakan, the hero of the epic *Civaka Cintamani,* disguised himself as an old man and wooed, by his music, a lady—Suramanjari—who had vowed never to even look at a man. When the women heard him sing, they rushed to him just like peacocks rush to the hunter who feigns the cry of a bird.

When I write about music that enchants, I remember an incident from my youth. Many scholars approached my Tamil teacher, Trisirapuram Mahavidwan Sri Meenakshi Sundaram Pillai, to get a prefatory poem from him. The great musician and Shiva devotee, Gopalakrishna Bharatiyar, wanted to obtain one for his Nandan Charitram, but Sri Pillai consistently refused. Yet Bharatiyar persisted. One day, when Sri Pillai was asleep inside, Gopalakrishna Bharatiyar, not wishing to disturb him, sat outside and started singing his work Nandan Charitram softly and sweetly.

When he sang "*kanagasabapathi darisanam kandal kali theerum*", Sri Pillai woke up and remained where he was, entranced in the song. He admitted it would be a mistake not to write an appreciation for this creation, and immediately wrote one. It is believed that Lord Shiva is an embodiment of music, and a lover of music. *Tevaram* describes him as *ezhisayai, isai ppayanai* that is Shiva is Music itself. We learn that in order to listen to music unceasingly. Shiva keeps two *gandharvas*, Kambala and Asvadhara, as his ear ornament, the *kuzhai.* The description of Shiva as "*isai virumbum koothanaar*" shows his partiality for music. *Tevaram* says,

"Emmirai nal veenai vasikkume", which means he plays the veena in hand with joy. This iconic form is called Veena Dakshinamoorthi. Is there anyone who is unaware of Krishna's flute spreading melody?

Many devotees have worshipped god by their music knowing that even god loves it, among them are the Nayanmars, Aanaya Nayanaar, Tirunaalaip Povaar Nayanar, Tiru Neelakanta Yaazhppaanar and Paramanaiye Paaduvaar. Aanaya Nayanar played the *panchakshara* on his flute and offered worship. *Paanapathirar* of Madurai played the *yazh* and worshipped Shiva. Lord Somasundara came down as a wood-cutter, and by his music defeated *Paanapathirar*'s challenger and made him run away in fright. Even among the devotees of Vishnu, we have Tiruppaanaazhvar, Nambaaduvan and other devotees.

The very fact that many of the prayers are in the form of melody shows that God loves music. *Tevaram, Tiruvachakam, Tirumurai, Tiruppugazh, Divya Prabandham* and *Tatuvarayar Paaduturai* are texts composed of songs. The *panns* of *Tevaram* were the creation of the aforesaid *Tiru Neelakanta Yazhppaanar*. The *panns* of *Divya Prabandham* must have also been created like this. Such books are called *Devagaanam*. Though now *Divya Prabandham* is sung in a tune that can be followed by everyone, originally each of the verse must have been set to a separate *pann*. In the *Divya Prabandham* texts now published they are set to many ragas that are not at all suitable. Each verse of a *pathigam* is set to a different raga. This is not correct.

We saw the greatness of music thus far. Now we will examine how the Tamils nurtured music.

The Music of the Tamils

In the Tamil Sangam of yore, they researched three kinds of Tamil (*iyal, isai and natakam*, or literature, music and drama). They excelled in research and practice of Tamil music.

Sangams of Tamil music were organized, and they were the centres for musicians to nurture Tamil music. Tiruchitrambala Kovai says, *Ezhisai soozhalpukkoí* reveals his love for music. Even among the poets of the last Sangam, there were musicians who authored research works. Among them are Kannaganaar, Kanna Naaganaar, Kesavanaar, Nannaaganaar, Nallacchuthanaar, Nannagannar, Pettaganaar, and Maruthuvan Nallacchuthanaar. There was also a Nedumpalli Aththanaar, and it is said that he was an expert in playing many instruments and perhaps, that is why he was called by that name. His songs refer to many instruments. At this juncture, the musician Pudukkottai Dasavadyam Krishna Iyer comes to my memory. He was an expert at playing ten instruments, and kept them all around him under a tent like structure and played on them.

In the last Sangam period, there were many books on the science and technique of Tamil music. These texts are lost and we only find references to them in some commentaries on *Silappatikaram*. The names of those books as gleaned from these texts are *Perunaarai, Perunkurugu,*

Pancha Bharateeyam, Isai Nunukkam, Panchamarabu, Tala Samudram, Kachhaputa Venba, Indirakaaliyam, Pathinaaru Padalam, Talavagai Oththu, Isaitamil Seyyuturai and Kovai. Books like *Suddananda Prakasam* came later and were also about music. Ancient literature about music are *Silappatikaram* and *Paripaadal. Silappatikaram* also speaks about the science of music. Even in books that came subsequently like *Civaka Cintamani, Choolamani, Kallaadam, Tiruvaaalavaayudaiyaar Tiruvilaiyaadal Puranam, Paranjothi Munivar Tiruvilaiyaadal, Athi Veera Rama Paandiyar's* books, some references to the science of music can be found.

Kuravanji, Pallu, Chindu and other later compositions are musical creations too.

We can surmise the extent of influence that music had from the fact that there were research books on music. I will now share what I have learnt from works like *Silappatikaram* about music.

Kinds of Music

There are two kinds of music *panns* and *thirams. Panns* had seven *narambus*.

Narambu means *swaram*. A *sampoorna* raga is one with seven *swarams*. This is a *pann*. This is called *melakartha* in Sanskrit. The seven *swarams* in Sanskrit are *shadja, rishaba, gandhara, madhyama, panchama daivata* and *nishada*. In Tamil, they are called *kural, thutham, kaikilai, uzhai, ili, vilari and thaaram*. The natural note for all of us is *shadjam*.

That it was called *kural* in Tamil is amazing. The seven *swarams* (*narambu*) are now taught as sa, ri, ga, ma, pa, dha, ni. In Tamil, they are pronounced as the long vowels, aa, ee, oo, yaay ai, o, au. I said earlier that a *pann* contains seven *narambus*, this is also the Janaka raga. From these the *thirams* were born or the Janya ragas.

In the *Divakara Sutra*, the character of *panns* and *thirams* is explained. *Thiram* was said to belong to *pann*. In *Yaapparunkalavrithi*, there is a verse which explains this. It is said that there are about 11,991 *panns* and *thirams* in total.

There are many *panns*. The five main ones or *perum panns* are *Kurinji, Paalai, Mullai, Marutham* and *Neidal*. There are many *panns*, some to be sung in morning, some at special times and hours. Morning *panns* are twelve, including *puraneermai*. Nine *panns* including Dakka Raga, are night *panns*. Three *panns*, including *Sevvazhi* are general *panns*. Some say that the morning *pann* is *Marutham* and the evening *pann* is *Sevvazhi*. Experts indicate certain things by these *panns*. A singer once sang a *malai pann* or an evening *pann* to indicate to his friend that they should meet in the evening!

Vilari is a *pann* that arouses compassion. A poet says that Ravana sang *Vilari* when he was crushed under the Mount Kailasha by Shiva to arouse Shiva's compassion. Poets sang such *panns*, composing lyrics, choosing the *pann* to suit the mood and the words. The *pann* and the words should blend with each other. Songs composed for *panns* were called *uru* and *vari*. The word "*uruppadi*" now used to refer to *kirtana*, must have come from the old word *uru*. Some say that there were ten kinds of *urus*: *Senthurai, Venturai, Perundevapani, Sirudevapani, Muththagam, Peruvannam, Aatruvari, Kaanalvari, Virimuran, Talaipogu and Mandilam.* Songs that were set to beat were nine: *Chindu, Tiripathai, Savalai, Samapada Vrithtam, Senthurai, Vendurai, Perundevapani, Sirudevapani* and *Vannam.*

Apart from this, there was one variety called *Gandharva Margam*, which was another name for the science of music. There were texts that set down rules for how to sing and the mistakes that had to be avoided. *Tiruvilayadal Puranam* mentions in a verse, some faults that a singer should avoid, like facial contortions, tremor and so on. Many of the faults can be seen in some celebrated singers. That is only because they have not corrected themselves.

Now let us look at musical instruments.

Musical Instruments

There were three kinds of instruments: *geethangam, nriththangam* and *ubhayangam.* The first named was to be used only when singing, the second only for plays and the third could be used in common. They mention the flute as the foremost of instruments, because this is closest to nature. When the wind blows through the holes made by bees in the bamboos, you hear a lovely sound. This natural melody is described in *Agananuru.* It is called *pullankuzhal* because it is made from bamboos. Some say that it is like the *kittippul* that children play with and hence the name. This is not correct. According to a text, bamboo is a kind of grass or *pul.*

That is why the flute got this name. It is also called *vankiyam.* That is derived from the Sanskrit word *vamsa* which means bamboo. The *Silappatikaram* describes the order in which the instruments came into existence, the flute, then the *yazh*, then *thannumai*, then the *moori*, and then *muzhavu.* Even the *tirukural* which describes the sweetness of the child's words mentions first the flute then the *yazh.*

There are many kinds of flutes, *konraiyan kuzhal, aambalan theen kuzhal, mullaiyan kuzhal* and more. These flutes are described and explained in many ancient books.

Similarly, there are many kinds of *yazh. Yazh* is different from veena. *Peri yazh* had twenty-one strings, *makara yazh* had nineteen and *chakora yazh* had fourteen, according to music books. *Senkotti yazh* had seven strings. They say that there was a *yazh* with thousand strings, called *aadhi yazh* and *perunkalam.*

These books explain the merits and defects of the string instruments.

There were many kinds of *thannumai*: *berigai, patakam, idakkai, urukkai, maththalam, sallikai, karadikai, thimilai, kudamuzha, thakkai, kanapparai, damarukam, thadaari, anthari, muzhavu, chandravaliyam, monthai, murasu, kanviduthoombu, nisaalam, thudumai, siruparai, adakkam, thaguniccham, viraleru, paaka, upaangam and nazhigaiparam* are leather instruments as seen from the musical texts. *Mathalam* is called that because of the sound that it produces. Like this, reasons are given for the names of the various musical instruments.

There were other instruments apart from those mentioned above, and we come across the mentions of instruments, like *aakuli, paandil, kodu, neduvankiyam, kurunthoombu, thattaiparai, pathalai and more.*

There were communities like Perumpaanar, Sirupaanar, Porunar, Koothar and so on, who learnt music and musical instruments hereditarily. They were patronized and rewarded by kings and wealthy men. The text *Malaipatukadaam,* describes them carrying these instruments, resembling a jack fruit tree laden with fruits.

The *paanar*s earned their livelihood by music. They sang before kings and chieftains and received gifts by their musical expertise. We learn that it was a custom to give golden lotus flowers as gifts. This is similar to the medals given to musicians today to honour them.

Sirupaanars were those who played a small *yazh*. And Perumpaanars played the bigger *yazh*. In big cities, there were streets designated for such musicians to reside.

My Experiences with Students

Preface

It is not easy to work in a university. Students would often try to annoy the teacher unless the teacher knows how to teach and also how to discipline. Students delight in pointing out the defects of their teacher. At the same time, if they form a good impression about their teacher, the love that they show is really special and they respect that teacher all their lives. Such a loving relationship between teachers and students is wonderful and it is this bond that makes the teacher's job so worthwhile; otherwise, it would only be drudgery. I worked in the Government Arts College, Kumbakonam, from 1880 to 1903, and from 1903 till 1919 in the Chennai Presidency College. By divine grace, I had the good fortune of working as a college professor for nearly forty years. Before I came to Kumbakonam, I was both a student and a teacher at the Tiruvavaduthurai *matha*. Even after I left Presidency College, I taught at the Sri Meenakshi College, Chidambaram. But my tenures in Kumbakonam and Chennai were most important for my service to Tamil.

The joyous scenes that I dream of are the times when I spent with students, while enjoying their enthusiasm and conversation. It is an unparalleled experience to be among carefree students who, totally forgetting their family, gather like birds in search of knowledge. My heart is recharged with energy, when I think of the affection shown by my students. These events happened many years ago, but they are still fresh in my memory. That is why I rejoice even today when I remember my days of teaching in the college.

The students of yesterday were not like today's students. They could appreciate what was good. They considered devotion to God, respect and humility as virtues. I consider it my good fortune that I had the opportunity to teach such students.

It is only natural that students will be playful and some even played pranks during class. But if disciplined properly, they can be immediately controlled like the snake is by the snake charmer. Then, they are filled with remorse for their acts. Even if their pranks are too serious, it would be a pity if the teacher punishes them harshly using their powers. On the contrary, if the teacher just deals with them as innocent pranks done without knowing what is proper, and guides them, they will show respect to the teacher.

I have never openly criticized the erring student. But I kept it in mind, and in some context during the class, I indicated that such wrong acts harmed the development of the students. Otherwise, I narrated to them a story and through that, showed such behavior as wrongful acts. After this, the guilty students came to me privately and sought pardon and promised to mend their ways.

Every teacher will be familiar with the strange pranks of students. I think it is better to call it a playful prank than a venomous, mischievous or stupid act. I am going to share some experiences that come to my mind.

Under "Loka"

When I joined the Kumbakonam College as a Tamil teacher, I succeeded Vidwan Sri Thyagaraja Chettiar who also taught me the methods he followed. Before that, I had never taught in an English educational institution. There are many differences between teaching in a *matha* and teaching in a college. When I taught, I made the students read the verse that had to be taught and briefly told them the meaning of that verse. After, that I explained the difficult terms. As far as possible, I made them recite these verses to music. I did not insist on those, who did not have musical training, to sing. I made them repeat the verse in such a way that each term was separately pronounced, making the meaning clear to everyone. It was my habit to start the new lesson every day, only after asking questions about the previous day's lesson. One day, I was teaching *Naidatham* in first year FA (First Examination in Arts; equivalent to Intermediate Arts or IA). *Indra Padalam* was prescribed for them. As usual, I began by asking questions about the previous day's class. One part of the verse contained the word "*andar ulagam*". I asked a student what the word meant. Without any hesitation he said, "The world of the Nagas." Even before I could hear him, the entire class burst into laughter. Some even covered their mouth, unable to control themselves. Everyone knew that this was the wrong answer. But I wondered why they were all laughing so much. The student who had replied stood there, puzzled. I gestured to the others to be quiet and I asked that student why he had answered so. He was totally confused and he blinked at the students and me in turn. Realizing that he was not going to give an explanation, another student said, "In English 'under' means what is beneath. I think he may have thought *andar ulagam* is the nether world." Only then it was clear to me. Then I explained that sometimes there may be terms in Tamil, which are a combination of Sanskrit and Tamil, but there was no likelihood of any word that combines English, and that *Naidatham* was written long before English came to this country and that its author had no connection with the colonial language.

After that, I told the students that when they study they must understand every word, they must understand how each word is derived and that one must not arbitrarily select some meaning. I also told them if there were Sanskrit words, they must go to the source and try to understand the meaning.

Pearls in the Fields

I once had to teach a verse from the Nadu Padalam in *Naidatham*. It was about the prosperity of Nidatha country and the generosity of its wealthy people. The gist of the verse was that the citizens of the country gave huge gifts of precious articles to the priests who were well-versed in the Vedas, and when they gave the gifts with the ceremonial offering of water, the water flowed and nourished the paddy fields, which were full of conches bearing many pearls that shone like the young moon. I explained the difficult words and the special features of this verse. All the students took notes. One student, aged about fourteen years, stood up.

"Why are you standing?"

"I have a doubt in the verse."

"Please tell me."

"The persons who come to receive gifts would have come to the city crossing the fields. Is it not? When that is so, they would have seen the pearls filling the fields. They could have easily taken them and made money by selling them. Why did they come to the city seeking gifts?"

I knew that he was a good boy and had a genuine doubt. I also realized that he may not have come across such descriptions before. So, I explained:

"The meaning of this verse is that there were many philanthropists in that kingdom. It is this that the poet describes so cleverly. It is poetic fancy. In grammar, this is called *uyarvu navirchi ani* (hyperbole). Even when we speak, we say something that is contrary to nature. We say a horse can run more than 100 miles an hour in praise of its speed. When speaking of somebody's immense capability, we sometimes say that he will swallow everyone. About a lucky person, we say whatever he touches becomes gold. Can we take the literal meaning of these words? If you say of someone that he will drink a big quantity of gruel without any salt, can you bring a drum of gruel and ask him to drink it? It only means that he would easily perform a task that would be very difficult for others. Similarly, poets use such descriptions. They speak of city walls being a fence for the Karpaga tree to indicate very high walls. When describing a city, if the coconut trees on either side of the road were very high, they would say that the feet of the sun's horses—as they galloped—tapped the coconuts, letting the tender coconut water flow on the road, making it muddy. Can you ask if it is possible to plant paddy in that mud? What the poet implies is that the coconut trees were lush and healthy. Such descriptions are found frequently in our literature."

The student then somewhat understood the meaning. But I was doubtful if he fully understood it. I also warned the students that it would not be correct to take the literal meaning and that it was necessary to understand what the poet really meant.

Our Ayya

Sri Thyagaraja Chettiar stayed in Mahathalam Pettai Street in Kumbakonam for a few months even after he retired from the college. Every day, after college hours, I went to his house in the afternoon and learnt from him. At that time, a part of *Naidatham* was prescribed for FA course. Chettiar had finished a portion of that when he retired, and I continued from that when I joined. As usual, one day I went to see him after college, accompanied by some students. Around the Mahamaham Tank, there are 16 beautiful Shiva temples built by Govinda Dikshithar. The one on the west was very convenient both to do *japam* and also to spend time in the evenings. Thyagaraja Chettiar was sitting there, teaching the *Tiru Idaikkazhi Murugan Pillaitamil* composed by Sri Meenakshi Sundaram Pillai to a student, Ramakrishna Pillai, we also sat there and listened to it. While explaining a verse, Chettiar cited a verse from Kamba Ramayana to explain it. He became totally immersed in Kamban words and was ecstatic. One of the students was P. Gopala Iyer who had passed BA first year, and was a resident on the western bank of Maha Maham Tank. Listening to Chettiar reciting the words from Kamba Ramayana and two or three verses thereafter, he praised and said, "*Ayya,* it feels so happy to listen to you teaching us these verses." Chettiar was pleased and he looked at me and asked, "Do you teach students like this so that the verses are imprinted in their minds and automatically they learn it by-heart?" I answered with humility, "What can I say? How can anybody teach like you? There is no comparison between us. I think of you while teaching. But I cannot teach like you." I could see that Chettiar was pleased.

One of the students who had come with me, who lived adjacent to Gopala Iyer, was Ramachandra Iyer, a very bold student who was studying FA. He cleared his throat and addressed Chettiar,

"*Ayya*, what did you say? You are posing a question which is very embarrassing to my *Ayya* in front of my own eyes. And he has also said that he cannot teach like you. It makes me feel very sad. When he joined college, you yourself said that he was very learned and a good teacher. After saying so, it is not proper that you asked such a question and that too before us. Our teacher teaches us very well, so that it is imprinted in our hearts."

"That is right, but does he teach so that you all remember it by-heart?" asked Chettiar.

"Do you think we don't? When he teaches, we learn the verses automatically by-heart."

"Is that so? Then will you recite some verses without looking at the book?"

"What is the problem? Please listen. I will recite."

After saying so, he started reciting some verses from 'Pirivuru Padalam' in *Naidatham*. Then he asked, "Is this enough or shall I recite some more?"

Chettiar did not leave it at that and asked him if he was not his student too, since Ramachandra Iyer had been taught by Chettiar for a while. Ramachandra replied, "Yes. But these verses have been taught by our *Ayya*. I may have forgotten some lessons that you taught us. But I have not forgotten anything that he taught us. He has taught us in such a way that we do not miss your absence and so that the place that you decorated is honoured. How can you ask such a question about our *Ayya*?"

"Can you ask your former master such questions so boldly?"

"Then, how can you say such things about our new master? I learnt this boldness only from you."

"What you say is right. It gives me great happiness that you praise the person that I appointed." Chettiar answered cleverly and laughed. I had been worried that having replaced Chettiar in the post of the teacher, what opinion the students would have of me. This incident comforted me and encouraged me.

Out of Portion Lesson

Two years after I joined the Kumbakonam College, one part of the book *Prabodha Chandrodayam* was prescribed for BA. It mentioned how Indra's body had become disfigured for the sin of desiring Ahalya. The version in this text was different from the versions in other texts. It was difficult to explain this verse to the students; so, I omitted this verse and explained all the other verses. I told them to ignore that verse and that it was vulgar and improper and that no question will be asked from that. I really thought that no question would be asked in the exam from this verse that ought not to have been included for study.

In those days, the BA examination was conducted only in Chennai. The Kumbakonam College students went to Chennai that year and wrote their exams. One of them sent the Tamil question paper by post, as soon as the examination was over. I saw that questions had been asked about that verse which I had omitted. It is impossible for me to express what I felt. I had joined the college only few years ago. I was anguished that I had committed a mistake and the students would find fault with me. I was also afraid what the principal would think of me if he got to know of this.

As soon as the students returned to Kumbakonam, ten of them came to meet me. I was convinced that they were coming to quarrel with me. What was done was done. How could I make amends?

When they came near, I said, "I have let you down. Even though the meaning of verse was inappropriate, it was my duty to have explained it. It was my misjudgement that I did not." The boys answered with a smile, "Please don't worry, sir. As soon as we saw the question paper, we guessed how anxious you would be. We came here in a hurry only to reassure you. We have no grievance that you did not teach us that verse. In fact, we answered that question much better than the other questions."

"How did you know the meaning?" I asked with surprise.

"Because you did not explain that verse, we knew that there must be something in it. We joined together and with the help of dictionary we learnt the meaning of every word. We asked the Sanskrit teacher and learnt about that episode. Please have no doubt, no one would have answered this question as well as we did!"

"Is that so? But still, it is my mistake that I did not teach you"

"Isn't it because you did not teach us that we focused our attention on this? So please don't think that you made a mistake."

I was grateful to God that it ended happily like this.

Aajanubahu

I was once teaching Kamba Ramayana, where Lord Rama has been described as one having long arms that reached his knees. This is considered to be a characteristic of a handsome male. Others, besides Rama, have also been described like this and the word in Sanskrit is *aajanubahu.* I told them by referring to other verses that such people were excellent in learning, valour and wealth, and had the ability to attract everyone easily. When I was explaining some special verses, I would always check if students were taking notes. I did so and observed that in one row where the boys were seated close to each other, the student who was seated in the corner had got up a little to see if his arm reached his knee. Obviously, he wanted to know if he had that indication of handsomeness.

"Is it to your satisfaction, my son?" I asked him.

He felt embarrassed and sat down. All the students laughed and from that day, they called him Aajanubahu.

Denuswasa Puram

Every year when new students joined the class, I asked them about their village, the special temples there and its history and so on. The students too were happy to talk about the greatness of their place. Some of the details I thus gathered are very rare and special. Once I asked a student from where he came and he answered

Denuswasa Puram. I had never heard of this place. So, I asked him where it was. He answered that it was in Kumbakonam Taluk.

I knew most of the towns in the Taluk, but I had never heard of Denuswasa Puram. I asked him "Is that so? I have never heard of it. Which is the town close to that place"?

"Near Aavoor."

"Near Aavoor? I have never heard such a town near Avoor and I know all the towns."

"It is Ootru Kadu."

I was puzzled because the student had made me think that it was some town unheard of.

"Oh? Is it Ootru Kadu? How did it get that name?"

"Kamadhenu worshipped Lord Shiva near Aavoor. Then it came to our town and exhaled. Therefore, it got the name Denuswasa Puram. It was first called Moochukkadu in Tamil and then it became Ootru Kadu." He explained. The whole class laughed and he frowned at them.

"I am very happy to hear these details about your town. If you had said Ootru Kadu right in the beginning I may not have asked you so many questions. You gave me the impression that it was some new town. That is how we came to know all these details. And I would not have been confused. You did not tell us the commonly used word, but the word used in purana. Maybe, your friends did not like that." I said that, referring only to the other students as his friends. They laughed again. From that day onwards, he was called Denuswasa Puram.

The Commentator Has Written it his Way

Once, I was teaching *Naladiar.* As usual, when I asked them questions about the previous day's lesson, one student gave an answer that was incorrect and irrelevant. I asked him why he was saying something incorrect and if he had not listened to the lessons on the previous day.

"I did not remember what you said yesterday. So, I read the commentary and this is what it says." As he said this, he gestured enthusiastically with the book in hand. His body language indicated that when the commentator himself had given this explanation, how I could have found fault with it.

"That is totally incorrect. But if it is like that, it has to be torn and thrown away. Come, let me see," I said, and he came quickly and confidently with the book in hand. All the students were also keen on knowing who the commentator was. The student who had come confidently up to my table, suddenly bent down. The confidence had gone. He looked as if he wanted to seek my forgiveness.

"I had not read the lessons. I am very sorry. I thought you would be afraid if I told you that the commentator had written so. That is why I seemed so confident. I will never repeat this," he said respectfully. I told him to study properly hereafter. He returned to his seat with his head bent.

Tervalan

In Kamba Ramayana Ayodhya Kandam, one verse describes Sumantra as Tervalan. I was explaining the term. 'Tervalan means someone who is a skilled charioteer like Sumantra.

He also was very good at giving advice like a good minister to the king. Therefore, this term is appropriate. The word 'Ter' as a verb as in 'Therthal' has been used," I said.

The students enjoyed this explanation as was evident from their faces. One of them was Govinda Rao, who was so happy that he said "*Ayya*, I like this explanation very much." I was happy to hear his wholehearted expression of joy and said, "I am happy to see that you listen to the lectures keenly. You will do very well in your life." About fifteen years after that, when Sri Ramachandra Thondaiman, the Pudukkottai Jaghirdar, was visiting Thanjavur, I went to meet him in his bungalow along with the well-known lawyer, Kalyana Sundar Iyer. Thondaiman saw us and welcomed us heartily. There was another gentleman with him, who looked at me and said, "Namaskaram." Looking at his appearance, his rich clothes and the bright earrings, I thought he might belong to the Maratha Royalty. I asked my friend who he was and I learnt that he was the personal secretary of the Jaghirdar. The secretary, who heard my question, said that he was my student. I could not recognize him.

"What is your name?"

"Govinda Rao."

"Oh, Tervalan?"

"Yes."

I was immensely pleased. The other two persons who were with us, were puzzled. I explained to them what had happened in college fifteen years ago. I said, "I often thought of him. Even then I knew he was very intelligent and had a bright future. Since I remembered him as he looked then, I could not recognize him now. I am sure he is a good counsellor to the Jaghirdar, like Sumantra, and so he can also be called Tervalan."

"Just as you have been thinking of me, I have been thinking of you. That day you blessed me that I will do very well. It is your blessing that brought me to this position," Govinda Rao said with gratitude and my heart was filled with joy.

Pride of One's Birthplace

When I was teaching Villiputhoorar's *Baratham* in the FA class, I had an occasion to speak about Tirukovalur. I was then working on publishing the *Purananuru*. I began to tell them some information and incidents from that text about that town.

"Tirukovalur is a very ancient town. During the Sangam period, there was a small chieftain called Malaiyaman Tirumudikkari. (He is one of the Kadai Ezhu Vallal or the last seven great philanthropists.) He was a great warrior. Whichever king he supported, Chera, Chola or Pandya, that king would win the battle. There was a forest called Mulloor Kanam near Tirukovalur. The ancient Tamil text praises Kapilar who was one of the great Sangam poets and lived in Tirukovalur during his last days. It is also a very famous sacred place being one of the Atta Veeratanam shrines special to Lord Shiva. It has a temple dedicated to Vishnu. The three first Alwars came there once at the same time and worshipped Vishnu." The students were listening intently to all this and one of them stood up. I thought he had some doubt and asked him why he was standing. He answered that Tirukovalur was his town and his face was radiant.

When even very wise people have extreme fondness for their place of birth, it is not surprising that it made their students very happy. I realized, that as I spoke of the greatness of Tirukovalur, he must have been so filled with enthusiasm, that he had to reveal that he came from that town; at that moment I stopped my lecture.

"Is that so? I am very happy. You must attain great fame that befits your town." And I looked at all the other students and said, they must have an affinity for their town like this student. I then proceeded with my lesson.

A Student's Objection

An extract from *Vinodarasamanjari* was prescribed in the syllabus. It contained an account of the atrocities of a Mohammedan ruler who had demolished temples and tormented his subjects. While the class was going on, a Muslim student stood up suddenly. "Is there no one to question this? The account is a calumny of that king."

He was a very polite and respectful student, but he could not tolerate the criticism about a person of his faith. The intense emotion made him burst out like this, forgetting that it was a class where there were many students and a teacher. He sounded like a person raising his objection amidst a large gathering, against an unjust accusation. I turned to him.

"Such lessons should not be included in the syllabus. When there are so many general topics, it is a grievous mistake to prescribe for study a topic that will hurt a particular group. This is concerned with history, and scholars must test if this is based on truth. Please do not be upset. You can be a person whom everyone loves. It is but natural for people to criticize someone who has committed wrongs. We must not think that the criticism is wrong, because that person belongs to our caste or our creed. The whole world hates a wrong-doer. Will we protect the flames in our home with our clothes?" With these words, I offered him some consolation.

Ganapati and Subramanian

Ganapati and Subramanian were classmates in BA, very intelligent and were good friends. Yet, in class they would always behave as though they were in conflict. Every day, one would blame the other. If one answered a question during class, the other found fault with it. I decided I must put an end to this.

On one occasion, while referring to Turaimangalam Sivaprakasa Swamigal, I said that he was considered to be a *karpanai kkalanjiam* (treasure house of imagination), and that he was capable of composing excellent verses. After that I explained to them one verse.

"Once when Shiva and Parvati were in Kailasha, Ganesha came to them crying, and stroking his ears with this trunk. Shiva asked him, 'Why are you crying?' His reply was that Subramania pinched him on his ears, and he began to cry more loudly. Shiva then summoned Subramania and asked him why he pinched Ganesha. He said angrily. Subramania said, 'But can he start counting how many eyes I have?' So, Shiva asked Ganesha, 'Why did you tease him?'

'Why should I be quiet if he starts measuring my trunk?' was the reply. Subramania stood laughing. Siva realized that his enquiry would go on endlessly. He looked at Parvati and said, 'Look at your sons!' At once Parvati said, 'Ignore him, he is very mischievous,' and comforted Ganesha."

I then recited the verse and said, "Obviously it is common for Ganapati and Subramania to quarrel, and as proof, we have these two students in our class." The whole class burst into laughter. The two stopped quarrelling from that day.

This Is Not Kumbakonam

I started teaching at Presidency College, Chennai, from 1 December 1903. Before I left Kumbakonam, people warned me that Chennai is a big city and the students cannot be disciplined. I left everything to God. Soon, I realized that what they had said was true. Chennai was modern and the students were very independent. They considered the teacher as a teaching machine and did not accord any respect. They were afraid of the principal and a few senior lecturers, but they treated the rest as they pleased.

Once, many students had come to write an examination. Sri Rao Bahadur M. Rangachariar, the head of the Desa

Bhasha pundits, was the person who had to distribute the question papers. The pundits and students waited for him to arrive. The students were shouting, laughing and banging the benches with their feet. Some students seated in the back row flung their caps, which were caught by the frontbenchers with their heads. Papers, books and pencils travelled by air from one hand to another.

I saw this chaos, and thought this must be a scene that specially characterizes the city of Chennai. Softly I asked one student, "Please be quiet, why do you shout?" He paid no heed to me, and retorted boldly, "You be quiet. This is how it is here; this is not Kumbakonam." I realized it was futile to continue the conversation. I hoped I could transform this to Kumbakonam one day. By God's grace, after some time, the students grew more obedient. Chennai too gave me as much satisfaction as Kumbakonam, and I was overjoyed because I taught more students in Chennai.

Timely Help

The day after the above incident, when I was taking class, a student in the front row had his right leg raised and resting on his left thigh, his knee held by both hands, and every now and then he was shaking his legs. He had no intention of listening to me. He had studied elsewhere earlier and had now joined here. He had never seen such splendid buildings and spacious structures ever before.

His attitude indicated to me that he was under the impression, it was his good fortune that he was a student here, and it was he alone and not his old classmates who was lucky to enjoy this sea-breeze and such facilities.

I was teaching Kamba Ramayana and just then it was the passage about Hanuman.

"Hanuman was valiant. He went to Ravana's court hall. Ravana was regally seated on a throne. He did not ask Hanuman to sit, nor did he offer him a seat. Hanuman noticed this and resolved to insult Ravana. By coiling his tail, round and round, he made a seat near Ravana that was taller than the throne. He leaped on it, and sat with one leg on the other, knees raised and arms wrapped around them. How can I clearly describe his posture? Look here, just like him."

And I pointed to that student. The class burst into laughter and it took several minutes for the mirth to subside. The student who was listening to my words like the others, was startled when it ended with him. He let his arms off his knees, and lowered his legs, and sat properly.

After the class was over, the students left for their next class. This student met me privately.

"How can you humiliate me like this?"

"Your appearance and your posture were very good. What is the point in me alone enjoying it? I thought everyone must see you. Moreover, your posture offered timely help, I could show you as a comparison. Otherwise, I would have been at a loss."

He departed silently. I think no one will doubt my comparison.

An Old Woman's Blessing

When I was teaching Villiputhuraar's *Bharatam,* I had an occasion to refer to the twelve names of Vishnu commencing from Kesava. I asked a Brahmin student.

"Do you know the twelve names? They are recited while doing Sandhyavandanam. If you do, please say them."

"I don't know them."

"Do you know the Achamana Mantra?"

"No."

Then I asked him to say some other mantras, he did not know them.

"Everyone must follow their traditional practices. It is essential that every human being should offer prayers at the appropriate time. Elders have set down appropriate practices for every religion and caste. If we follow them, divine grace will bless us. *Sandhya vandanam* is a kind of prayer too. If it is done regularly, one's memory and intelligence will become sharp." After these words, the lesson continued.

Some days later, the boy whom I had asked about *sandhya vandana* mantras met me after college.

"My father has been wanting to meet you for some days now. Please come home." I agreed, since his house was on my way home from college. His father welcomed me and offered some snacks. He had been my student in Kumbakonam.

At that moment, an old lady peeped from the kitchen. When the father saw her, he pointed to me and said, "He is the one."

I was startled. I did not know why he pointed to me like that. I was afraid if I had earned their disapproval in some way. Seeing the confusion in my eyes, the boy's father said, "That is my elder sister. For some time now, my son is doing the *sandhya vandanam* regularly. He has got his own *panchapatram*, *uthrani* and *vibhuti* bag. Previously, my sister had told him so many times to do it, but he did not listen at all. It saddened her. Suddenly, one day, he asked Sastrigal to come home and teach him the mantras, and since then he is doing it. Our surprise knew no bounds. We asked him how wisdom had suddenly dawned. He said, 'We have a new Tamil lecturer; he asks us about *sandhya vandanam* and other mantras. And he also said I must not fail to do it.' My sister has been blessing you since then, and she has been saying, 'Is there such a person these days? I want to see him at least once.' That is why I asked my son to invite you home."

"Many boys are staying here, away from their parents, in order to study. The parents will be under the impression that their children are doing well. There is no one who is concerned about them here. It is the teacher alone who should care. These days, some people may not approve of what I did. But since I do it for the students' good, I do not care about their opinion. I am very gratified that at least some like you approve of my action."

The old woman sent a child with a tray with fruits and *tamboolam* for me.

Restraint on Speech

One day, two students were chatting with each other, paying no attention during class. I pointedly looked at them, but they did not notice me. So, I stopped teaching and remained silent. The other students did not know why, and a student in the front row requested me to continue with the lesson.

"I could do that, but those two are talking about something very interesting. I think I should not be a distraction to them. Maybe they live far away, and if the matter is something very important, they cannot come this far again, right? Moreover, there is no time like now to converse; with the pleasant sea breeze blowing, they are chatting. Even if I do not help them, I must not be a hindrance to them. That is why I have stopped." Then I looked at them and asked, "Will you take some more time?" Their faces were like two drooping lotuses among the several blooming ones. I continued my lessons.

Durairaja's Chair

Sri Subramania Durairaja, one of the younger brothers of the Raja of Pudukkottai, studied in our college. On the instructions of the principal, a special chair was kept for him in the class room. And he sat there.

Once a student realized that Durairaja would be absent for some days, and so, as soon as he entered the class, he sat on the special chair. The students and I noticed it. The students grumbled at him.

The next day, he came dressed in expensive clothes to look like Durairaja. He thought his attire must match the seat. It looked as if he had long nurtured a desire to sit on that chair. He came rushing to the place, but the chair was not to be found. He was disappointed and he searched for it all around.

"What is it? Have you dropped something? What are you searching for?" I asked him as I was in the classroom then.

Before he could answer, another student, Narayanaswami, replied. "He is searching for the chair."

I knew what had happened, but I pretended I knew nothing.

"Chair? Which chair?"

"Durairaja's chair. He thought he could sit there like yesterday; so, he is searching for it."

"Is that so? Where is it?"

"It is safe. It will return when Durairaja returns. When all of us are seated in our seats, why should this person alone want that chair? Is it fair to sit on somebody else's chair?"

"I agree. The principal himself has ordered that a special chair should be given to Durairaja. He belongs to a royal family. Can everyone insist on a chair for themselves? Further do you come here to sit on a chair, or to listen to lessons? Can you learn only if you sit on a chair? Today, he has come all dressed to sit on that chair. But it is alright. He may go and sit in the usual place."

When I said this, that student went quietly and sat down.

The Student Who Wore a *Namam*

One day, the lesson contained some information about wearing *vibuthi* on the forehead. I told the students that Hindus should not leave their foreheads bare.

The next day, I started the roll call before commencing the class. When I called the name of a Smartha boy, the one who answered seemed different. He was wearing a bright *tiruman* or *namam*.

"Why are you answering instead of him?" I asked him.

"I am that person."

I noticed him carefully.

"Oh, really? But you are wearing a *namam*, why? I asked him.

"Yesterday, you said that everyone should wear their mark on their foreheads, is it not?"

"So, did you do this yourself? Or did somebody else apply it for you?"

"He was the one who put the *namam* for me." And he pointed to the other student. Everyone laughed.

"What you did is not correct. Everyone should wear only that mark which they are expected to wear. You should do what your elders do. I got confused that instead of you, an Iyengar student had come. But in one way, what you did was right. At least you realized that you must wear the mark on the forehead. That is enough."

From that day, he wore the appropriate mark on his forehead.

Tell Me the Rasam

Once I was teaching the students the part where Dronacharya is mourning Aswathama's death. Before reciting those verses, I told the students about the greatness and knowledge of Villiputhur Alwar.

"This is full of rasa," I said.

"Did you see the rasa in these verses? There are thousands of such verses in Tamil. In my opinion, there is nothing that gives more joy than to savour the sweetness of Tamil."

After the class was over, all the students went out except one. He was sitting there, pencil in hand with his notebook looking at me as though he was waiting to write something.

"Why are you sitting here?" I asked him.

"You said that the verse contains rasa, I am waiting for you to say what rasa?"

I controlled my laughter. Is the rasa in a verse like lemon *rasam*?

I did not know what to say and then I told him, "This *rasam* we have to understand and enjoy with our intelligence. We cannot write or read about it. As your love and study of Tamil increases, you yourself will understand the rasa."

He must have been disappointed that there was nothing for him to write down. But what could I do!

Sons-in-law

There were many men who criticized their sons-in-law who were my students in college. They were under the impression that I could make them improve. I realized the expenditure and anxiety that was caused by the sons-in-law.

During a lesson, I had the opportunity to speak about sons-in-law.

"I feel very sad when I think of some sons-in-law of today. Those who are studying in college, not content with the money that they receive from their father, also write to their fathers-in-law and spend that money wastefully. In fact, they write to the fathers-in-law in an authoritative and threatening tone. I am sure none of you will do that. I just want to tell you what is happening in this world." I noticed that two students in the back row were talking to each other.

"I know what you are saying. You must be saying that this teacher has been harassed by his sons-in-law. Is it not?"

They agreed.

"What you thought was wrong. I don't have any daughters. But I know many fathers-in-law and they tell me about such matters. I thought that if I told you, you will not get such a bad name."

Pallavi Raga

I often insisted on the students to learn the verses with music. I would encourage those who had a melodious voice, and I would also sing in different ragas as a demonstration. Whenever I said that verses must be learnt with music, some students would point to another saying that he can sing very well. I told them, "Singing kirtans and ragas alone should be described as singing and *sangita vidwans* sing like that. If you recite verses with a tune that cannot be called singing, nor can a person who has learnt that become a *sangita vidwan*. The Tamil verses have been composed in such a way that it is suitable to recite them with a tune. And when you do so, you will know the tonal excellence of those verses. In the grammar of verses or *seyyul ilakkanam*, the word *seer* means *talam* or rhythm. Those verses which have been set to a tune like music are called *seer*. All of you must try to repeat the verses with the tune at least to some extent."

I thus taught them not to refer to this recitation with a tune as singing.

One day, I read out some *virutham* in different *ragas*. I told the students to name any raga that they knew and that I would recite in that raga. Each of them named ragas that they knew and I was reciting the *viruthams* accordingly. One student suddenly said, "*Pallavi raga*." All the students who knew a little bit of music laughed out, and so did I. That student was confused and did not understand why we were laughing. He must have thought, "When our teacher recited the verses in the ragas named by other students, why is he just laughing when I named a raga?"

"Do you know why they are all laughing?" I asked him.

"No. I don't know."

"*Pallavi* is not the name of a raga. The first part of a *kirtanam* is called *pallavi*. Every kirtan has a *pallavi*."

"But they use the words '*pallavi* singing', is it not?"

"That means singing the *pallavi* in different ways by changing the musical phrases and expanding the treatment of the raga. Some *vidwan*s are famous for singing like that. *Pallavi* Gopala Iyer is one such. That is why they laughed when you said *Pallavi Raga*."

Glossary

aadishaivar: one group among Shaiva initiates

adappaikaran: a person engaged to prepare *paan*

adey: like "hey"

agraharam: the streets where Brahmins lived

alankaram: a genre of Tamil poetry

archana: a form of worship to the deity consists of the deity's various appellations

ayya: sir

chombu: metal water pot

gnanadesikar: a teacher in a Shaiva math

japa: reciting the name of god repeatedly

kalambakam: a genre of Tamil poetry

kandhiar padal: Kandhiar is the name of the Jain Sanyasini Padal is songs

kolam: decoration made with riceflour on the ground like rangoli

mahamai: right to receive the share of the harvest or any other income

mahavidwan: great scholar

mandirikkovai: a genre of Tamil poetry

matha: monastery; here, Shaivite monastery

odhanavunum: cooked rice

naidatham: the story of Nala and Damyanti by Athiviraramapandiyan

paati: grandmother, or while addressing an elderly woman

pial: a raised platform in front of the house where people sat

samasthanam: a princely state

sandhya vandhanam: a ritual performed by reciting the Gayatri mantra; a small vessel, *panchapatram*, and a small spoon, *uthrani*, are used for this

shruti: in this context, it is the pitch

srotriyam: a kind of endowment

sthalapurana: the history of the temple

suddhamathalam: a percussion instrument

tamboolam: tobacco (here, for chewing)

thambiran: non-Brahman monk of Shaivite mutts of Tamil region

thavasi: cook

thinnai: same as *pial*, a raised platform in front of the house where people sat

thoda: a golden ornament like bracelet

tiruman, namam: a mark on the forehead shaped like a "Y" or "U" with a red vertical line in the centre worn by Vaishnavites representing Lakshmi and Vishnu

tiruvandikappu: a special evening ritual of worship in the Tiruvarur temple

ula: a genre of Tamil poetry

vana: forest

venba: a form of classical Tamil poetry

vibhuti: sacred ash worn on the forehead by Shaivites usually

vidwan: expert

vidyadhara: a demi god

yappilakanam: a book on prosody

yazh: a stringed instrument